CONTEST FOR EMPIRE
1500–1775

CONTEST FOR EMPIRE

1500-1775

PROCEEDINGS OF AN INDIANA
AMERICAN REVOLUTION BICENTENNIAL SYMPOSIUM

Thrall's Opera House
New Harmony, Indiana
May 16 and 17, 1975

edited by
JOHN B. ELLIOTT

Indianapolis
Indiana Historical Society
1975

This Indiana American Revolution Bicentennial Symposium was
sponsored by the Indiana American Revolution Bicentennial
Commission, the Indiana Historical Society, Indiana State University
Evansville, New Harmony Memorial Commission, and Harmonie
Associates of New Harmony, Indiana.

Copies of these *Proceedings* are for sale by the Indiana Historical
Society, 140 N. Senate Avenue, Indianapolis, Indiana, 46204,
for $2.00 per copy.

CONTENTS

PROGRAM

(All sessions held in Thrall's Opera House)

FRIDAY, May 16, 1975

2:00 P.M.   Presiding: John B. Elliott, Symposium Director and President of Harmonie Associates

Greetings: The Hon. Robert D. Orr, Lieutenant Governor of Indiana

Keynote Address: "Agents of Empire in Colonial America" George M. Waller, Chairman, Department of History, Butler University

Presiding: John L. Cotter, National Park Service Archaeologist and Professor of American Civilization, University of Pennsylvania

"The Impact of the European Presence on Indian Culture" James A. Brown, Professor of Anthropology, Northwestern University

8:00 P.M.   Presiding: Donald E. Pitzer, Chairman, History Department, Indiana State University Evansville

"Spanish Indian Policy and the Struggle for Empire in the Southeast, 1513–1776" John J. TePaske, Professor of History, Duke University

"The 'Rising French Empire' in the Ohio Valley and Old Northwest: The 'Dreaded Juncture of the French Settlements in Canada with those of Louisiana' " George A. Rawlyk, Chairman, Graduate Studies in History, Queens University, Kingston, Ontario, Canada

SATURDAY, May 17, 1975

9:30 A.M.   Presiding: Donald F. Carmony, Professor of History, Indiana University

vii

"Britain and the Ohio Valley, 1760–1775: The Search for Alternatives in a Revolutionary Era"
Jack M. Sosin, Professor of History, University of Nebraska

Presiding: Hubert H. Hawkins, Director, Indiana Historical Bureau

"The Advance of the Anglo-American Frontier, 1700–1783"
Thomas D. Clark, Professor Emeritus of History, Indiana University

2:30 P.M. Panel Discussion

Presiding: Donald F. Carmony

Participants: James A. Brown, Thomas D. Clark, John L. Cotter, Donald E. Pitzer, George A. Rawlyk, Jack M. Sosin, and John J. TePaske

8:00 P.M. Concert

Choral-Ayres, Dennis M. Sheppard, Director, School of Music, University of Evansville

PREFACE

John B. Elliott

The observance of the American Revolution Bicentennial has greatest relevancy when focused on regional activities of a historical nature, even though they may have been peripheral to the main theater of action. The less dramatic events occurring in the American hinterland during the pre-Revolutionary epoch have not received from historians the degree of attention lavished on events in the more populous eastern seaboard. However, it was the efforts of Western European powers to extend their overseas empires into the Ohio Valley and the Old Northwest during the sixteenth, seventeenth, and eighteenth centuries that led to a classic frontier confrontation. Colliding with each other and with powerful aboriginal peoples, these nations soon felt the pressure of the westering colonists. The offstage wilderness struggles that ensued involved small-scale skirmishes and competition for trading hegemony, but the outcome shaped the destiny of America's heartland.

Recognition of the importance of the events leading up to the American Revolution in the West generated the collaboration of five Indiana agencies to mount a historical symposium in New Harmony on May 16 and 17, 1975. Generous funding and counseling were provided by the Indiana American Revolution Bicentennial Commission and the Indiana Historical Society. Services in kind and personnel were furnished by Indiana State University Evansville, the New Harmony Memorial Commission, and Harmonie Associates, Inc.

The Symposia Committee of the Indiana American Revolution Bicentennial Commission envisioned a series of historical conferences to be held throughout the state; the first, in New Harmony, to serve as a pilot. To establish historical sequence and prepare the way for subsequent meetings, the New Harmony sessions dealt with the period between 1500 and 1775 as it pertained to events transpiring in the trans-Appalachian region. "Contest for Empire," emerged as the con-

John B. Elliott, Conference Director, is President of Harmonie Associates of New Harmony, Indiana, and Adjunct Professor of Anthropology, Indiana State University Evansville.

ference title. Historic Thrall's Opera House was the scene of the two-day symposium. Two hundred and fifty registrants in attendance comprised a broad spectrum of academic and lay people.

The conference was opened by Lieutenant Governor Robert D. Orr, chairman pro tem of the Indiana American Revolution Bicentennial Commission, and George M. Waller, chairman of the history department of Butler University. Governor Orr extended the official greetings from the State, and perceptively noted the propriety of launching the first major observance in the historic environs of New Harmony, a community with a long tradition of intellectual inquiry. Cogently, he pointed out that the Harmonists, who settled here in 1814, were no further removed in time from the Revolution than we are today from World War II—in both instances, a span of years within vivid living memory. Dr. Waller's keynote address, "Agents of Empire in Colonial America," proffered an encapsulated preview that foreshadowed much of the discrete data expanded and refined by the principal papers which followed.

The five papers by scholarly specialists presented in these proceedings treat respectively the transmontane interests and activities of the Indians, the Spanish, the French, the British, and the American colonists. Prepared independently, the papers fit together with fortuitous coherence in time and space.

In "The Impact of the European Presence on Indian Culture," James A. Brown presents an anthropologist's analysis of the historical events accompanying the European influx which profoundly altered all facets of life for native peoples as they sought to accommodate to a cataclysmic rate of cultural change. He clearly reveals the effects of Western European expansion upon the newly opened world of primitive man: deculturation, demoralization, depopulation, and defeat.

"Spanish Indian Policy and the Contest for Empire in the Southeast, 1513–1776," by John J. TePaske, examines the imperial role of Spain east of the Mississippi River, in an area marginal to, but impinging upon, the Old Northwest. Spain wavered between the use of force and the relatively humane policy of missionization employed by the Church; but she failed to hold Indian loyalties because of her inability to match the attractions of abundant and cheap trade goods available from the neighboring pragmatic British colonists. Lightly committed in this area from the beginning, she withdrew from the southeast borderlands to attend her more central interests in Mexico and South America.

George A. Rawlyk deals with "The 'Rising French Empire' in the Ohio Valley and Old Northwest: The 'Dreaded Juncture of the French Settlements in Canada with those of Louisiana.'" Unsuccessful in the search for precious metals, the French penetration became based upon the economic foundation of the fur trade. Their behavior and attitudes toward native peoples shared similarities with those of the Spanish: a paternalistic Indian policy, a dilute and unthreatening infiltration by Europeans, little disturbance of Indian land tenure, Christianization, and a mild cultural impact on native societies. France shared with Spain the competitive disadvantages of insufficient Indian trade goods, an advantage enjoyed in abundance by Britain, who was a hundred years ahead of the other powers in industrialization and who controlled the seas. Power on the Indian frontier was a product of Indian loyalties insured by supporting Indian economic dependence.

"Britain and the Ohio Valley, 1760–1775: The Search for Alternatives in a Revolutionary Era," by Jack M. Sosin, is an examination of British policy and activity on the frontier following the extinction of French and Spanish claims. Stabilization of the frontier required regulation of the Indian trade and the garrisoning of outposts, both dependent upon adequate financing. Reluctant to bear this load alone, Britain sought assistance from the colonies through levies of provincial troops, cost-sharing through the notorious stamp duties, and restriction of white encroachment on Indian lands. Failure to achieve any of these objectives resulted in the British abandonment or weakening of outposts as the growing turbulence on the eastern seaboard required an expanded military presence there. As a concomitant of the military withdrawal, administrative responsibility for Indian affairs was surrendered to the ineffectual colonies, further destabilizing the frontier as the Revolution approached.

"The Advance of the Anglo-American Frontier, 1700–1783," by Thomas D. Clark, recounts the inexorable, disorganized, westward movement of a mass of humanity comprised of hunters, pioneers, traders, and settlers into the trans-Appalachian region. This sweeping encroachment on Indian lands instituted a new level of white-Indian relations in scale and intensity. Ineffectually restrained by governmental policy or action, the momentum created by this westward movement of a colonial people would not halt until it had spent itself at the Pacific coastline. Indian policy, as practiced by the American government, became one of dispossession and eviction through thinly disguised ameliorating treaties.

The conference concluded with a concert of appropriate seventeenth- and eighteenth-century instrumental and choral music presented by the Choral-Ayres of the University of Evansville under the direction of Dennis M. Sheppard. A musical work by Peter Pelham, the Williamsburg ancestor of an old New Harmony family, was featured.

The Director is indebted to a number of individuals for dedicated assistance in planning and executing this conference. Foremost are

Donald F. Carmony, professor of history at Indiana University, who served as liaison between the State Commission and the Director, presided over several sessions, and rendered invaluable publicity service through the pages of the *Indiana Magazine of History*, and Donald E. Pitzer, chairman of the history department at Indiana State University Evansville, who helped with the planning throughout the effort and led a symposium section. Hubert Hawkins, director of the Indiana Historical Bureau and editor of the *Indiana History Bulletin*, chaired a session and lent publicity assistance through his publication. John L. Cotter, professor of American civilization at the University of Pennsylvania, presided over the Friday afternoon session with wit and informed comment. Through the good offices of David L. Rice, president of Indiana State University Evansville, the recording services of the Instructional Media Center were provided; and with the help of Judy Rogers, secretary to the president, copy was prepared and printed by the university's printing office. Gayle Thornbrough, director of publications for the Indiana Historical Society, supervised the several phases of preparation for publication of these proceedings by the Society, and was most helpful with editorial direction. My wife, Josephine M. Elliott, deserves unmeasured credit for the help she gave every step of the way.

Clement B. Penrose VII, staff artist for Historic New Harmony, Inc., deserves special mention for drawing the symposium symbol. It was adapted from an Indian peace treaty medallion shown in Karl Bodmer's *Bildatlas*, which accompanied the travel book of Alexander Philipp Maximilian, Prinz von Wied-Neuwied, *Travels in the Interior of North America* (1843). It is reproduced on the cover.

The Director hopes that the tenor and content of the New Harmony Symposium will prove an inspiration to those that follow, and quoting Dr. Waller's comments on the major papers, "Out of their knowledge of the past we may hope to draw perspectives on the present and directions for the future."

NEW HARMONY, INDIANA
July 28, 1975

CONTEST FOR EMPIRE
1500–1775

Agents of Empire in Colonial America

George M. Waller

It is appropriate that we meet during National Historic Preservation Week for this first symposium of the Indiana Bicentennial. New Harmony is a gratifying success story in the preservation of significant sites of our history. It is also a place remarkable for its beauty at this season as springtime spreads its greenery and blossoms. We appreciate that, too.

The speakers at this symposium are all specialists. Out of their knowledge of the past we may hope to draw perspectives on the present and directions for the future. Our sessions are, therefore, in the full spirit of the Bicentennial, which celebrates not only our heritage but also seeks to recognize the accomplishments of this nation, born in 1776, as it stands today, and our hopes for its future.

Our subject, "Contest for Empire," spanning a period of three hundred years before the Revolution, acknowledges that the American Revolution as it was fought in the Mississippi and Ohio valleys involved rivalry among Britain, the new United States, France, Spain, and the Indians. All had a stake in the region. All had occupied or dreamed of occupying these rich lands west of the Appalachians since the seventeenth century or earlier. All had contended for the area before the Revolution and continued to jockey for advantage during the War for Independence and for years afterward. During the war these five forces employed both military and diplomatic efforts that were only a continuation and intensification of similar efforts to develop and hold an empire in America's heartland that they had pursued consistently, though sometimes sporadically, for a hundred years.

The story of this contest involves a diversified series of events and a constantly shifting cast of characters. Men and actions marking the

---

George M. Waller, a specialist in colonial American history, is chairman of the Department of History, Political Science, and Geography, Butler University.

I

imperial struggles here in the West are usually submerged in our historical accounts by more crucial struggles for empire in the zones of friction along the eastern borders; New York and New England with French Canada, southern British colonies with Spain, expansionists from the upper South and middle English colonies with Indians, and clashes of commercial and fishing interests in the western Atlantic Ocean. By comparison, the clash of empires in the transmontane region was small scale. Though highly significant, many events have attracted only passing mention from the historian, escaping analysis frequently because they got lost in the sweep of romantic narrative, as in Parkman's great history. Sometimes, for example, in the accounts of Spanish and French colonies, events in the Ohio and Mississippi valleys have been relegated to a minor role compared with activities of those imperial efforts in South and Central America, the Caribbean, or Canada. One concludes, also, that few recent historians have delved into early moves on this far-removed chessboard of empire.

The speakers at this symposium are outstanding among those who have been taking another look at the trans-Appalachian West in the years before the Revolution. They will be analyzing for you developments in the contest for empire that laid the basis for a series of culminations, of which the Revolution was only one. Earlier, Britain's victory over France in 1763 had changed the nature of the contest. Later, the continuing struggle was marked by the mysterious intrigues of Genêt, Wilkinson, Burr, and others, the diplomacy of Jay and Pinckney, the Louisiana Purchase negotiations, and the War of 1812.

In speaking of five "empires" represented in the Ohio and Mississippi valleys in the years before the Revolution, we are defining "empire" figuratively and broadly, as a state having an extent of territory and a variety of people. Three were well-established, centrally ruled European nations: Britain, France, and Spain. One, represented by partially self-governing North American settlers, was to become the United States. The fifth, to stretch a point, was made up of Indian tribes, constituting not at all a "state" in the European meaning, decentralized to an extreme, but presumably sharing a common interest in the contest for empire with the other four.

But it would be a mistake to assume that each of these five represents a unity arrayed against the others. Each had within it different interest groups. With each, the dominant policies as well as the goals of sub-groups vacillated in successive time periods. Hence, objectives shifted for each empire and for those interests represented within each.

Each speaker will be dealing with his protagonist in his own way. I seek only to set the stage. Those who follow will discuss the discrete issues they have found to be important in the confrontation here in the West in the formative years.

The agents of empire were many and various as were their activities in pursuit of imperial goals, and just as often, if the truth be told, of their own personal objectives. Each area had its own composite: Spanish, French, British, as did the Indians, although with them factors operated in a more primitive way.

Obvious among the agents of empire are the early explorers. Add to them the royal governors (and the Indian leaders). Each government had its apparatus of superintendents of Indian affairs and Indian agents; these in turn often worked closely with trappers and traders. The church hierarchy, represented in the wilderness by priests and missionaries, advanced the cause of state as well as church. Soldiers on expeditions or in garrison were highly visible agents of empire, regulars, volunteers, or militia. Surveyors for land speculators vied with actual frontier settlers in the imperial march. Often overlooked are the mapmakers, frequently government or military agents. Early maps and knowledge of their makers tell us much about the visions of empire and the values put on particular areas. A contest for empire implies acquaintance with territory that can be imparted to associates, a kind of knowledge best conveyed by maps. Even Indians made maps to aid in their movements.

Except for a few great explorers or colonial governors, who do we know today of the legions of agents who served their kings in these western lands? To suggest a few would only betray my own limited knowledge. May we hope that our speakers will rescue for us some of the most important though forgotten agents of empire and the goals they sought, men whose service for their states or tribes significantly shaped the future?

Agencies of empire also include institutions. Our speakers will doubtless be touching upon governments with their legal systems, land policies, and religious establishments. Business, education, and social and cultural patterns mark the thrust of each empire into the wilderness representing vast potential for conflict with rival patterns.

On all the agents of empire and agencies certain obstacles imposed themselves. Distances and wild terrain were problems to all engaged in the contest, though to some extent favoring the Indian, because of his life style, over the European. That all were handicapped by the clash of goals among traders, land speculators, and settlers has long been recognized, and all were disadvantaged further by official policies that sometimes ran counter to the interests of all three. Indians, too, were divided between leaders favoring accommodation with the whites in the interest of trade and those conservators of heritage, territory, and custom who opposed all white advance.

So many questions may be raised about this contest for empire, and so many contradictions observed. If our sessions here deal with only some of the problems, and end up raising more questions than they answer, so much the better; our occasion will have been well served.

For example, what, we may ask, did the French want with the region? French settlers of the Illinois country, as it was called, made little use of the rich lands of the Wabash and Mississippi valleys, to the often-expressed disgust of English observers. Farming only enough to support themselves meagerly, and for that utilizing Negro and Indian slave labor, French inhabitants were devoted to Indian trade and a leisurely existence, a debauched life in the eyes of more rigidly disciplined Anglo-Saxons.

What of Spain after 1764, contenting itself with small outposts on the west bank of the Mississippi before, yet resurrecting claims to both banks and eastward to the Ohio River during the Revolution, and pursuing these claims with military gestures and diplomatic demands?

What of differences in Indian policy? The British controlled the tribes by lavish gifts; the American settlers only by force of arms and numbers. Yet the French and Spanish, too poor to bribe the Indians and too few to awe them, gained Indian love and Indian trade.

What was the British purpose? Possessed of the Ohio Valley and the whole Northwest after 1763, Britain hesitated and vacillated, clearly unsure of where to place authority or what laws and institutions to introduce. It abandoned military posts and reduced garrisons, miserably failing to enforce the Proclamation Line, while white settlers drifted west even beyond the Ohio, and highly placed gentlemen in London flirted with land speculators from the colonies.

We need to know more of official aims, if indeed they can be deduced from the broad generalities often uttered. Edmund Burke's "to turn a savage wilderness into a glorious empire" is a trumpet call to the contest, but what does it mean? Was Adam Smith closer to the mark for the British in suggesting they "found a great empire for the sole purpose of raising up a people of customers" for his nation of shopkeepers?

With a glance over our shoulder at recent events, perhaps we should rejoice that none of the contestants in the western lands was strong enough to fulfill the foreboding definition of an ancient Greek man of wisdom, "To plunder, to slaughter, to steal; these things they misname empire, and where they make a desert, they call it peace." But to the Indians, the ultimate losers, this was very near the meaning of empire and the outcome of "peace."

In the end, the contest for empire was won in the Ohio Valley, at least for the moment, at the end of the Revolution, as it had been waged down through the years, by the persistence of woefully small bands of fighting men, usually lacking adequate supplies. They were volunteers and militia drafts led by officers sprung from the ranks rather than high-ranking regular officers.

It was lost by inadvertance and lack of responsible direction and leadership. All along it had been a wilderness struggle enacted offstage and far from the centers of government. Men, military and otherwise, had labored hard, endured neglect, obscured by the problems, pressing or petty that preoccupied their imperial masters and left them and the empire in the West far from uppermost in the thoughts of European ministries.

But in a larger sense, the contest at this stage was won by force of numbers—the steady flow of people moving westward, huddled in forts, tilling their fields with guns at their sides, suffering indescribable hardships, cruelties, and starvation. As Daniel Boone wrote, "We can scarcely behold a spot of earth but what reminds us of the fall of some fellow adventurer massacred by savage hands. Our number of militia is decreased. Our widows and orphans are numerous. Our officers and worthiest men fall a sacrifice."

Still, the people came all through the war years, a force the imperial treaty makers could not realistically ignore, men and women of the new United States launching an imperial march to the Pacific against which neither the scattered British outposts, nor a few French and Spanish villages, nor unorganized, erratic Indian leadership would stand.

The Impact of the European Presence on Indian Culture

JAMES A. BROWN

INTRODUCTION

In recounting the contest for empire in the Old Northwest native Americans all too readily can be relegated to a dependent role in shaping events. If we were to take the historical record at face value, their history would seem to be one of defensive reaction—not creative action. As DeVoto stated in an oft-cited criticism of frontier history, "most American history has been written as if history were a function solely of white culture."[1] There is no disputing the point that the European presence was dominant from the time of its first permanent foothold on the continent. What can be lost sight of are the diverse complexities of Indian cultural adjustments to European intrusion, especially since few Europeans had any in-depth understanding of native cultures. Fortunately, modern scholarship has provided us with a more detailed and balanced perspective on native Indian culture through a combination of historical, ethnological, and archaeological studies. The resulting composite contradicts the customary notion that Indian adaptations in the historic period were a simple defensive reaction to the presence of European culture. Although future research will considerably amplify our knowledge, I would like to review some of the important known dimensions of aboriginal culture change in the Old Northwest. Before doing so it should be made clear that there was an inevitability to the outcome of the territorial contest between natives and Europeans. As long as European nations were growing in population and extending their economic systems overseas, their eventual domination of the North American continent was not in doubt.[2] What happened historically in the area of the Old Northwest and Ohio Valley before 1775 turns out

James A. Brown, a leading theoretical anthropologist, is Professor of Anthropology, Northwestern University, Evanston, Illinois.

upon examination to be very similar to other conquests by empire-building nations. The same type of event has been repeated many times over on other continents during the eighteenth and nineteenth centuries.[3]

INDIAN POPULATIONS

To begin my review I think that the matter of Indian population size is signally important. The numbers of native Americans occupying the Old Northwest prior to 1775 will probably turn out to be the single most important factor in the history of European conquest. Numbers were so recognized at the time, since estimates of warrior strength were avidly collected by Europeans concerned with monitoring Indian movements and military potential. In their estimation of their own future in North America Europeans were correct: their domination crucially depended on the relative numbers of Indians and Europeans.

When Europeans had penetrated the Great Lakes area in the seventeenth century, they met a numerous population whose relative density was to affect the course of Anglo-French rivalries for over one hundred years. Here was the densest population of interior North America north of the Deep South during the seventeenth century. This concentration was massed in a belt running eastward from the Detroit region across the lower Great Lakes and into the upper St. Lawrence Valley, the Finger Lakes region of present-day New York, and the upper Susquehanna Valley. The majority of the village-dwelling polities situated in this band were Iroquoian-speaking.[4] Surrounding regions were more sparsely settled. To the north lay the cold coniferous forests of low population potential, and to the south small populations were concentrated in relatively few villages despite the greater population potential of the vast territory of the Ohio Valley and the Illinois country. The Shawnee tribe occupied a portion of the Ohio Valley and the Illinois and Miami tribes held the Illinois country.[5] Farther south in the Mississippi lowlands the population was concentrated in a few villages. At the northern end dwelled the greatly reduced Quapaw.[6]

No greater contrast to the sizable population in the southwestern-Ontario-to-New York belt existed in the seventeenth century than the population void in the warm fertile riverine valleys of the Ohio, Wabash, Illinois, and Mississippi.[7] By prehistoric standards these heartlands of early river-valley agriculture below the glaciated terrains were population voids.[8] The reason may be readily available from what we know to be the effects of Old World diseases upon New World peoples. Ample opportunity existed for epidemic die-offs to affect native population. When de Soto made his famous journey in 1542 deep into present-day Arkansas, his men made contact with many tribes in the most densely settled portion of interior North America. Their density made them highly vulnerable, and indeed when the French returned one hundred and thirty years later the Mississippi Valley above Vicksburg was virtually deserted. There is certainly a strong contrast between the Indian populations encountered by de Soto's men in their march through the Mississippi Valley and the paltry numbers found by Marquette in 1673.[9] Mass migrations are not involved since those tribes that remained are known from archaeological evidence to have their roots in the valley, and there are no other tribes extant that can trace their origins to this area. Instead archaeological evidence on the remnant tribes points to rapid cultural change in the direction of decreasing complexity of social and political organization. The cause of this decline can most readily be attributed to population losses.[10]

The Iroquoian-speaking groups and their neighbors were adequately insulated from the population crashes of the Southeast for the very reason that their population growth was relatively recent. They did not sustain heavy interaction with the town and village tribes of the Southeast before the mid-sixteenth century. Nor did the Iroquois peoples reach their population apogee until later since density-induced social stress only occurred about the time of contact.[11] The effect of a population depression in the older, densely settled portions of the mid-continent was to remove from the contests for European domination in the seventeenth and eighteenth centuries the very centers of organized political life that gave de Soto difficulty in the sixteenth. However, improved agricultural efficiency to the north in the area of Upper Canada and neighboring New York was presumably the factor behind the continual rise in population that crested in the seventeenth century. The very area of swelling population was in the region of initial French, British, and Dutch colonial settlements.

Populations there did not remain high for long. Smallpox and warfare soon made severe inroads that eventually affected native capability to cope with expanding demands on their lands by increased numbers of Europeans. Smallpox epidemics scourged the Huron from 1636 on. The Iroquoian tribes were hit as early as 1649, and by the end of the century at the close of the Iroquois War native populations had dropped by more than half.[12] Similarly devastating epidemics ripped through Indian settlements during the eighteenth century.[13]

Disease was only one side of the mortality picture. Alcohol combined with bad nutrition in general, which is invariably found in its company, was an equally strong depressant on population.[14] Aboriginal adjustment to these conditions varied according to circumstance and their organizational ability to cope with them. The League of the Iroquois in its heyday kept well ahead of population attrition by incorporation of defeated peoples. But warfare in the eighteenth century failed to provide for the Iroquois the numbers necessary to maintain a steady population. Other tribes in their dependence on the fur trade system were worse off because they were inadequately organized and hence they fell easy prey to debilitating and chronic health problems.[15]

THE REGION

The other developments in the contest depend on a geographical background to reveal the real diversity of environmental potential to the low-yield energy requirements of native American cultural systems. The Old Northwest is simply a large triangular tract bounded by the three major waterways important historically to travel through the mid-continent. Sweeping across this territory are distinct natural environments with strikingly different potentialities for human exploitation. They have structured human life-ways and continue to do so. The potentialities of the Great Lakes region, in contrast with those of the Illinois country and Ohio Valley, were sufficiently appreciated by the French from discovery to have influenced planning and policy.[16] Agriculture was more successful in the floodplains fingering out from the Mississippi lowlands. It is in these lands that aboriginal populations concentrated in prehistoric times.[17] On the other hand, trapping was more productive of first-class pelts in the colder, mixed hardwood-coniferous forests in the North, precisely in those lands where corn agriculture was risky if not entirely impractical during periods of cold climate. It was in these lands that the fur trade system promoted by coureurs de bois and the merchants of New France dominated economically. In the Upper Great Lakes the impact of the fur trade promoted cultural developments not sustainable through traditional aboriginal economies.[18]

THE FUR TRADE

The fur trade which so completely enmeshed Indian cultural life into dependence on the metropolitan economies of France and later Great Britain actually went through several stages of development, each with its own character. Long before the peoples of the mid-continent came into the orbit of historical observation, the European presence had made its impact.[19] European hardware and beads were being traded into the Great Lakes hinterland far in advance of French penetration. The new materials merely traveled along traditional networks of inter-group exchange and by so doing created a demand for European trade goods that threatened and later supplanted traditional valuables. In the exchanges ritual gift giving, as known through such important social events as Feast of the Dead ceremonies, was an aboriginal vehicle.[20] However, hardware and other artifacts were not the sole items to advance beyond the frontier of European discovery. Useful subsistence plants rapidly diffused. A European plant, the watermelon, came to be grown in the Illinois country before the Illinois had contact with the French. The watermelon was of Spanish origin out of the Southwest or the Gulf Coast.[21] As for the European role, we can characterize it as unorganized. Before 1663 the French fur trade around the Great Lakes was a relatively simply organized system with a primitive logistics.[22] Visits were sporadic and expeditions were uncontrolled by central authority. The high travel risk of the ventures and the low population of European adventurers combined to keep the expeditions as small scale, intermittent entrepreneurial enterprise. But when Canada became a royal colony, expansionist policies were inaugurated that indirectly encouraged by 1667 the increase in the volume of fur returned to France. Soon the increased number of traders led to the circumvention of the Ottawa middlemen who represented the interface between aboriginal and European trade networks, and a larger number of European trading expeditions penetrated the Great Lakes and the Illinois country on a more frequent basis. The Ohio Valley itself remained outside of this expansion since it was dominated militarily by the Iroquois to the point that they held exclusive trapping rights to the area. Also, it is suspected that they uprooted most of the resident population from the area and dispersed it. The Iroquois were obviously not relying on a middleman role in their adjustments to the European presence.

Although the expeditions of Marquette and La Salle brought the Illinois country clearly within the French trading orbit, the Canadian authorities were unable to back up these explorations which had greatly increased the fur trade clientage among tribes south of the Great Lakes. The Canadian organization was really incapable of sustaining military support in such far removed regions. Soon, however, the onset of French and Iroquois hostilities led to increased metropolitan support for the scattered posts in the trading hinterland. The result of this support was the investiture in 1683 of these posts with small garrisons. Their military commanders soon proved to form effective linkages in an administrative chain reaching from each isolated post to the king's ministry.[23] So effective was increased involvement of French interests in the hinterland that it led unwittingly to overproduction through a greatly expanded fur trade. The quick glut of the market that ensued forced the king to curtail the trade in order to protect through stringent regulations the fur trade income. The regulations essentially reduced trade without sacrificing the military organization or its administration and without significantly reducing access to the Illinois country. In fact during this period trading was centralized out of Detroit for about a dozen years by concentrating sizable portions of the Illinois country tribes in the vicinity. Considering the attractions of European patronage, mere persuasion by the French was sufficient to relocate so many tribes. The stresses both to the trading system and to intertribal relations, however, made this arrangement fragile and futile. Nonetheless, the fact that it endured as long as it did for so many of the mid-continental tribes testifies to the degree to which they were dependent on the fur-trade system.

With the recovery of the fur trade in 1714 the old organization was expanded, and the reliance on the existing military command organization was extended by the leasing of the post trade to military commanders.[24] French organization in the Old Northwest was growing by significant degrees. Hence by the first quarter of the eighteenth century the overhead of operating the trade network began to intrude conspicuously. The effect of leasing was to disadvantage Indians trading at leased posts whether leases were held by commandants or merchant farmers. Prices to the Indians increased, but the threat of Anglo-American trade in better quality goods at lower prices led to the rescinding of the leasing practice in the Old Northwest by 1749. The effect of almost sixty-five years of centralized administration and licensed control of official trade was a steady rise in prices and a corresponding increased dependency of native trade on licensed posts. The scope of the dependency was amply demonstrated in 1747 during King George's War when a combination of naval blockade and the fall of Fortress Louisbourg interrupted the trade supply line with devastating results. Increasing scarcity of trade goods and spiraling prices threatened to precipitate an Indian uprising throughout the Northwest; tension was only relieved with the arrival of supply boats from France in 1748.[25] The Indian reaction was a harbinger of things to come when the British unwisely exercised false economy in the New World after winning the war with France.

The competition with the English propelled the French trade empire into expansion and, as a consequence, into greater organizational complexity. The bold expansion of the trade into the hinterland beyond Lake Winnipeg necessitated establishing intermediary distribution posts with satellite support communities.[26] Accordingly, around 1740 Fort Michilimackinac was upgraded to a distribution center for the northern posts and Detroit was built up as the corresponding southern entrepôt. In addition the latter carried the burden of provisioning the former. As a consequence, limited European settlement in the wilderness was encouraged.[27] During the same century scattered settlements were established in several strategic positions in the Old Northwest. Such French communities served as centers of French and Indian rapprochement in some cases and as symbols of irritation in others.[28]

The amount of French and English competition can be gauged by the fact that during the above-mentioned war a sufficient number of traders began to pour from Pennsylvania that by 1749 three hundred Anglo-American traders were reported in the upper Ohio Valley.[29] The French reacted to the competitive threat by a show of force and the founding of a chain of military outposts along the main trails between the Upper Ohio and the Great Lakes.

The final showdown between French and British interests in the Seven Years War revealed the extent to which the British had economically outstripped the French. The army the British fielded to the New World was much larger than any other power had been able to support heretofore, and the forces it left behind served to consolidate British administrative control over the new territories. The army was an expenditure that Great Britain could consider seriously due to her greatly enhanced economic position, the result of increased productivity from the Industrial Revolution. The British greatly strengthened their logistic network with improved transportation and augmented bureaucracy.[30] Cheap trade goods continued to be sold, and more importantly, the British were able to absorb a higher-sustained fur trade.[31] Otherwise, the old organization remained intact until personnel were gradually changed and licensing became open to larger numbers of traders.[32] The effect was to deepen Indian commitment to supplying furs in exchange for hardware and dry goods.

But soon after the British triumphed over the French, they instituted a policy of curtailing gift giving in ignorance of its role in maintaining aboriginal societies in the Ohio Valley. The result was a region-wide uprising known as Pontiac's War.[33] Though there were several factors contributing to this war, the withholding of gifts must stand as one of the principal causes. The cessation of hostilities brought a resumption in the flow of gifts.[34]

EFFECTS ON SETTLEMENT

From the beginning of direct European contact the fur trade altered aboriginal settlement locations and continued to be a determining factor in tribal political geography up to the end of the eighteenth century. It was the location of trading depots that was particularly influential on aboriginal locational strategies because there was freedom to move around in the mid-continent in the fur trade period due to low density of human settlement.[35] French interests in collecting tribes around their trading posts were seemingly matched if not exceeded by corresponding eagerness of Indians to cluster around them for advantageous trading purposes.[36] However, in every case where more than one tribe was involved such clustering severely taxed the native political organizations to cope with such unaccustomed close contact.[37] Moreover, population clustering occurred even where the subsistence economies in the more northern posts were inadequate.[38] Hence such aggregations were impermanent. But up to the time of the Fox wars, at least, such aggregations were attempted, motivated the founding of the Detroit settlement as much by reasons of administrative economy in the trade as they were motivated by the desire of native groups to consolidate monopoly among Indian clients.[39] With the crushing of the Fox in 1734, middleman monopoly practices within the aboriginal trade network seem to have disappeared as a feature of the trade in the Old Northwest. Indians became simply clients of European traders. Only the Five Nations held onto their former control of Indian clients[40] and this hold declined at a steady rate during the eighteenth century.

A second effect of the fur trade, and the European presence as a whole, can be seen in tribal dislocations and ethnic "extinctions." We are ignorant of the effect of the initial European discoveries of the sixteenth century in the St. Lawrence Valley and in the Southeast on Ohio Valley and Illinois country tribes. When history reaches the Great Lakes area and its hinterland, tribes were already on the move and attempting to escape from the depredations of the Iroquois war machine on the one hand and the particularly effective raiding of the Sioux on the other.[41] Many of the Central Algonkian tribes that later became important in the history of the Midwest were dispersed at this period from an aboriginal homeland in eastern Michigan, presumably at the western end of the densely populated belt of the lower Great Lakes.[42]

The principal force behind tribal dislocation was the power that access to guns conferred. The more eastern tribes held a natural advantage in being close to European suppliers, but some measure of relief to the inland tribes was afforded to the weak power position of the latter by contact with isolated trading parties. For the Ohio Valley and Great Lakes peoples it was the military might of the League of the Iroquois that was feared. In the competition for hegemony following European contact it was the League and its constituent tribes that were triumphant. Specifically, the Seneca were able to drive out and beat their rival Iroquoian-speaking tribes in the Niagara Frontier region before the League took on the Huron in 1649 and destroyed the tribes around the southern shore of Lake Erie by 1654.[43] In 1656 the League's force was felt as far away as the Illinois country. At this time the League held uncontested hegemony among the remaining independent tribes in the Northern Appalachians, the Great Lakes, and Ohio Valley.[44] The League's rise to dominance took less than twenty years. It maintained its dominance for about one hundred years through repeated military expeditions. The Iroquois reputation for fierceness was well deserved since they swept all tribes before them that were not incorporated through adoption. But their reputation was not due to some inherent ferocity. Rather it followed from their organizational capacity for war. To them the maintenance of repeated war expeditions happened to be an organized solution to intertribal relationships among the Five Nations. At the close of Iroquoian hegemony in the Ohio Valley, the League established client relations with resident tribes by allocating them territory and by appointing over them "half-kings."[45] By the 1740s, however, the Anglo-American influence in the Upper Ohio had exceeded the critical level of balance maintained heretofore.[46]

SOCIAL AND POLITICAL CHANGE

Indian involvement in the fur trade brought about marked changes in native social and political organizations throughout the Old Northwest. The small totemic-named bands that were sprinkled through the northern hardwood and coniferous forests at the fisheries of the upper Great Lakes were politically simple societies until the fur trade swept them into the quest for beaver and a higher level of economic security than attainable through aboriginable subsistence. The first multi-band aggregation to take place in this region congregated at the Falls of St. Mary's. Soon it was replaced by the first large Chippewa village at Chequemogan on Lake Superior, which was more strategic to the fur trade.[47] Thus the Chippewa arose from the aggregations of formerly isolated small totemic kindreds into a tribal organization. The maintenance of this village of one thousand was a novel development in this life zone that changed the political complexion of the upper Great Lakes.[48] French fur trade depots elsewhere led to much larger populations, which the tribally organized constituents were neither accustomed to nor capable of accommodating to, on a long-term basis. The Illinois, for example, maintained a large village on the shores of Lake Peoria during the 1680s containing members of all the subtribes while the remaining constituents of these divisions continued to maintain their normally semi-independent ways.[49] Such novel aggregations thrust new forms of political integration on Indian societies that in the Midwest were generally organized for autonomy and expansion through warfare.[50] A contrary development took place among tribes with greater political concentration by the relinquishing of tribal authority to band organizations that assumed more autonomy than they had heretofore (e.g., Winnebago).[51]

As a result of Indian demand for trade goods a decided shift in aboriginal work budgets took place. Fur trapping gained at the expense of traditional hunting and fishing as adult male tasks. With the change came a shift in settlement patterns from larger village aggregations to smaller more isolated communities. Political activity became even more acephalous. Traditional underpinnings of tribal unity became significantly eroded.[52]

So far the fur trade can be shown to have had only long-term, atomizing effects on Indian societies. However, the European presence in the seventeenth century also stimulated intertribal competitive pressures that effected major transformations in the formation of confederations such as the League of the Iroquois out of formerly autonomous tribes.[53] League formation among the Iroquoian-speaking peoples is a relatively recent development that arose almost simultaneously among the Hurons, the Five Nations, and the Susquehanna.[54] Whatever the benefits confederation brought to the Hurons and others, their attempts at solving the threats to social stability that the centuries of population growth brought them by the seventeenth century were less successful in the final showdown than was the League of the Iroquois. Among all, the novel political organization of confederacies developed to halt the threat of blood feuds among its tribal members.[55] But the Five Nations found it far easier to funnel intra-group aggression into large-scale military expeditions than to subvert the more desirable atmosphere of mutual confidence. Hence their successful solution to internal civil control led them to displace civil strife with external warfare. Warfare to them was a means for maintaining political stability.[56] Little wonder that Iroquoian warfare has been so little understood.

RELIGIOUS CHANGES

Christian missionaries were a major instrument of culture change during the French and British regimes. Beginning with the Jesuit conversions in the Great Lakes area and Illinois country and ending with protestant missionaries in the Anglo-American colonies, native Americans were induced to take up Christianity through the efforts of both organized and unorganized missionary activity. Early successes were heavily influenced by the overawing circumstances of early missionary contact. Though Jesuits thought of their successes as springing from religious superiority, it is obvious from the contexts of conversion that Christianity had strong overtones of a political and economic nature to aboriginal populations. Conversion appears to have been an act inspired by the desire to establish a patron-client relationship, which endured as long as social and political conflicts did not disrupt it. Large numbers of Indians throughout the area came to be attached to mission settlements. Many intermarriages with French traders took place that helped swell the port populations and provide a stable work force in the fur-trade system. In the Northwest the "mixed bloods" did not constitute a simple class or ethnic group, but rather they affiliated with either the French population or Indian tribes, probably depending on the social standing of the couple and their children.[57] Conversion and subsequent association with a mission were acts that were equally political and religious.

The sustained effect of missionary activity in the Old Northwest was to alter subtly the cultural milieu of native religious thought. Despite the fact that both personal vision quests and priestly ceremonies retained their essentially aboriginal function in tribal social organizations, Christian themes and notions began to insinuate themselves into aboriginal thought. The effect of missionary work and contact with Anglo-American culture can be felt in the content of the Delaware Prophet's message. This revivalistic movement among the Delawares in the 1760s was the first of several important nativistic movements that upwelled among the easternmost native populations.[58] Though the Prophet's message did not sustain an enduring cult or religious movement, it seems to have inspired more significant movements later, one of which was to have lasting effect on Iroquois life. What is important here is the degree to which Christian ideology and symbols had been injected into a consciously native movement that attempted to return Indians to the true faith of the ancestors.[59]

Religious change encompassed far more than the customarily held belief that such change was acceptance or rejection of active missionizing effort. Rather, the character of, and even organization of, aboriginal ceremonial can be shown to have adjusted to the European presence, specifically through the altered economies and the new social and political dependencies fostered by the fur trade. The Midewiwin among the Chippewa and other Central Algonkian and Siouan tribes who adopted the ceremony from the Chippewa has been shown to have emerged as a specific ceremony in the period of early impact of the fur trade of the Great Lakes in the seventeenth century.[60] First given historical notice in Raudot's memoir (1709-10) as an organized shamanistic cult which deals essentially with the death and rebirth of victims, the Mide ceremony came to be performed by its initiates in the large aggregated settlements that grew up in response to the fur trade or under active direction of French leaders.[61] The Mide ceremony served to bind in common participation tribal populations among some Central Algonkian and Dakota Sioux that were unaccustomed to joint social action and had relatively ineffective political governance. Hence it was a socially integrative device that evolved among peoples lacking formal political structures to accommodate their societies to the stresses of increased population aggregations that resulted from the various forms of involvement in the European fur-trade system.

MATERIAL CHANGES

The most apparent and striking change in Indian life, irrespective of specific culture brought about by the European presence, was the replacement of aboriginal tools and containers by European products. The hardware, dry goods, and decorative items the Europeans could produce and trade were eagerly welcomed from the very beginning of contact; indeed they were probably received in limited numbers well in advance of personal contact with the white man. At any rate, Indian demand for these trade goods promoted an active trade with Europeans that was initially realized by Ohio Valley tribes through Indian intermediaries and then through direct contacts with European traders.[62] Their most valuable exchange commodity was beaver peltry although other furs were recognized as of value at different periods. When the market for pelts collapsed (as it did briefly between 1695 and 1714) or declined (as it did in the southern areas without rebounding), the demand for trade goods did not abate; rather, it was the same or more intense. The dependence of native Americans on hardware especially (decorative items secondarily and clothing or dry goods tertiarily) was complete. Note that all aboriginal mid-eighteenth century sites contain little pottery and except for some evidence of aboriginal flint technology, iron and brass hardware has replaced all flint products.

The gap between Indian supply of beaver and Indian demand for European products was made up largely by gifts. For some tribes and bands local conditions allowed high pelt production or its equivalent in another valued commodity. A case in point is the production of a maize staple for provisioning locally stationed French (and later British) soldiers.[63] Indian trapping, hunting, and agriculture was productive, but native demand for goods easily outstripped their means of acquiring them through the productivity of the local economy. It is easy to see how it could, once it is realized that usage was not restricted to ordinary utilitarian demands since only so many iron and brass kettles, guns, axes, knives, etc., can be used per capita. Rather, hardware and beads were used to sustain a trade into the hinterland, and items of all classes were conspicuously used in mortuary rites and passed out of circulation through interment with the dead. European traders decried the latter usage at first, but they were unable to prevent it since aboriginal status systems were dependent upon the destruction of valued goods on important social occasions.[64] Actually, Europeans willingly co-operated with this intrinsic Indian demand by bidding for Indian allegiance through Indian gifts.[65] When the British stopped gift giving on the customary scale after the removal of French competition, the reaction was formidable and nearly universal throughout the area.

PATTERNS OF INTERTRIBAL RELATIONS

The European presence on the Atlantic Coast and on the St. Lawrence River brought about a change in intertribal relationships. Previously, the dominant polities that occupied the Southeast maintained intracontinental trading patterns that were largely north-south from the Gulf of Mexico to the Great Lakes area[66] (where the primary aboriginal commodities of marine shell and native copper were localized respectively). The waning of the southeastern populations, and the growth in the populations around the Great Lakes and far East, helped to change this aboriginal *realpolitik*. However, European presence clinched the development by sealing the dominance of the Iroquoian-speaking peoples over midwestern tribes. One cannot speak of intertribal relationships in the Ohio Valley and the Illinois country without reference to the League of the Iroquois since the League was able to exercise a degree of political influence through the mid-continent that was unmatched in historic times. In their creative use of warfare they were not unique. Rather, they were applying time-honored means for creating an orbit of political control that worked to maintain internal population strength, while maintaining the trading-distributional network. In this role they were both respected and feared by the Ohio Valley tribes.

Outside of the Iroquoian sphere of political control the effects of Iroquoian domination and intertribal jockeying for privileged middleman standing created a political crisis that required a mechanism for maintaining forms of intertribal peace. The form that evolved was the calumet ceremony which created a bond of sacred kinship that was likened to a passport by European observers.[67] Its original sphere of recognition was the Old Northwest and beyond to the west into the Plains and south into the Caddoan lands, but it swept through the Midwest by the 1660s.[68] As a means of cementing alliances the calumet ceremony had its competitor among the Iroquois in their practice of presentation of wampum belts. Only after Iroquois hegemony had been effectively compromised in 1751 in a confrontation with the Miami did the Iroquois themselves recognize the validity of the dance as a means for maintaining intertribal peace.[69]

CONCLUSION

It used to be popular to depict the Ohio Valley Indian as either a blood-thirsty savage or as a child of nature disrupted from his isolation by the European discoverer. Neither of these images is true since native Americans were never such one-sided peoples. Rather, they adhered to their self-interest throughout, and they took political stances and waged war for reasons that served that interest. Competition among tribes and desire for booty were the bases for warfare among all except the Iroquois who also employed warfare as a means for internal solidarity. Throughout the period of the fur trade aboriginal culture in its technological, social, and ideological aspects was adjusting to the crises brought about by involvement in the fur trade, the presence of European military forces, and the pressures of European settlers. Aboriginal capabilities were limited, of course, but these limitations were largely dependent on small tribal size and the low population densities among them—densities that were continually being clipped back through disease, warfare, and other forces.

The outcome of the contest for domination over the Old Northwest was decided by transplanted European cultural systems, but the European presence significantly restructured intertribal relationships and helped bring the unusual Iroquois culture to the fore. In all, native American peoples resisted European domination in a manner consonant with aboriginal cultural forms and to the degree that their small-scale social systems would allow.

NOTES

1. Bernard DeVoto, "Joseph Kinsey Howard," in Joseph Kinsey Howard, *Strange Empire: A Narrative of the Northwest* (New York: William Morrow & Co., 1952), pp. 8–9, cited by Lewis O. Saum, *The Fur Trader and the Indian* (Seattle: University of Washington Press, 1965), p. ix, and by A. Irving Hallowell, "The Backwash of the Frontier: The Impact of the Indian on American Culture," in *The Frontier in Perspective*, edited by Walker D. Wyman and Clifton B. Kroeber (Madison: University of Wisconsin Press, 1957), pp. 229–58, who tried to redress the inequity. Another good example of history from the Indian position is contained in Nancy O. Lurie, "Indian Cultural Adjustment to European Civilization," in *Seventeenth Century America: Essays in Colonial History*, edited by James Morton Smith (Chapel Hill: University of North Carolina Press, 1959), pp. 33–60.

2. See Kingsley Davis, "The Migration of Human Population," in *Scientific American*, CCXXXI, No. 3 (1974), pp. 92–105.

3. David K. Fieldhouse, *The Colonial Empires: A Comparative Survey from the Eighteenth Century* (London: George Weidenfeld & Nicolson, 1966); Wilbur R. Jacobs, *Dispossessing the American Indian: Indians and Whites on the Colonial Frontier* (New York: Charles Scribner's Sons, 1972).

4. Bernard G. Hoffman, "Ancient Tribes Revisited: A Summary of Indian Distribution and Movement in the Northeastern United States from 1534 to 1779. Parts I–III," in *Ethnohistory*, XIV (1967), 1–46.

5. For a discussion of historical evidence on Shawnee locations before the Iroquois depredations of the 1670s see James B. Griffin, *The Fort Ancient Aspect* . . . (Ann Arbor: University of Michigan Press, 1943), pp. 11–35. More recent research may be found in John Witthoft and William A. Hunter, "The Seventeenth-Century Origin of the Shawnee," in *Ethnohistory*, II (1955), 42–57. The Illinois and Miami locations at contact are reviewed by Wayne C. Temple, *Indian Villages of the Illinois Country: Historic Tribes* (Illinois State Museum, *Scientific Papers*, II, Pt. 2, Springfield, 1958).

6. Antoine S. Le Page du Pratz, *The History of Louisiana* . . . (Reprinted. Baton Rouge, La.: Claitor's Publishing Division, 1972), p. 303. Ethnohistoric information has been reviewed by Philip Phillips, James A. Ford, and James B. Griffin, *Archaeological Survey in the Lower Mississippi Alluvial Valley, 1940–1947* (Robert S. Peabody Foundation for Archaeology, *Papers*, XXV, Andover, Mass., 1951), pp. 392–421. The Quapaw are almost certainly the Pahaca of de Soto. See Jeffrey P. Brain, Alan Toth, and Antonio Rodriguez-Buckingham, "Ethnohistoric Archaeology and the De Soto Entrada into the Lower Mississippi Valley," in *The Conference on Historic Site Archaeology Papers*, VII, 232–89 (Wilmington, N.C., 1974).

7. Hoffman, "Ancient Tribes Revisited," in *Ethnohistory*, XIV, 1–46. For a map of Iroquoian-speaking tribes of the contact period see Bruce G. Trigger, *The Huron Farmers of the North* (*Case Studies in Cultural Anthropology*. New York: Holt, Rinehart & Winston, 1969), frontispiece.

8. See James B. Griffin, "Eastern North American Archaeology: A Summary," in *Science*, CLVI (1967), 175–91, for an up-to-date overview of the archaeology. Depopulation is handled in Henry F. Dobyns, "Estimating Aboriginal American Population," in *Current Anthropology*, VII (1966), 395–416.

9. John R. Swanton, *The Indians of the Southeastern United States* (Bureau of American Ethnology, *Bulletin 137*, Washington, D.C., 1946), pp. 11–14.

10. Continuity in the lower valley has been summarized archaeologically by Philip Phillips, *Archaeological Survey in the Lower Yazoo Basin, Mississippi, 1949–1955* (Robert S. Peabody Foundation for Archaeology, *Papers*, LX, Andover, Mass., 1970), pp. 923–54. The archaeological context of the de Soto contact has been established by Brain *et al.*, "Ethnohistoric Archaeology and the De Soto Entrada into the Lower Mississippi Valley," in *The Conference on Historic Site Archaeology Papers*, VII, 232–89.

11. The historical context for the formation of the League of the Iroquois is argued by Elisabeth Tooker, "The Iroquois Defeat of the Huron: A Review of Causes," in *Pennsylvania Archaeologist*, XXXIII (1963), 120. A slightly earlier dating was favored by Anthony F. C. Wallace, "The Dekanawideh Myth Analyzed as the Record of a Revitalization Movement," in *Ethnohistory*, V (1958), 118–30. Archaeological evidence for the stresses leading to the confederation is developed by Robert Whallon, "Investigations of Late Prehistoric Social Organization in New York State," in *New Perspectives in Archeology*, edited by S. R. and L. R. Binford (Chicago: Aldine Publishing Co., 1968), pp. 223–44, and Whallon, "Rim Diameter, Vessel Volume and Economic Prehistory," in *Michigan Academician*, XI, No. 2, pp. 89–98.

12. E. Wagner Stearn and Allen E. Stearn, *The Effect of Smallpox on the Destiny of the Amerindian* (Boston: Bruce Humphries, Inc., 1945); William J. Eccles, *The Canadian Frontier, 1534–1760* (New York: Holt, Rinehart & Winston,

1969), pp. 122, 124, 125. For an example of Iroquois depopulation see Edmund B. O'Callaghan (ed.), *Documents Relative to the Colonial History of the State of New York* (15 volumes. Albany, N.Y., 1856–87), IV, 337–38, IX, 129, 492; and Reuben G. Thwaites (ed.), *The Jesuit Relations, and Allied Documents* . . . (73 volumes. Cleveland: Burrow Brothers Co., 1896–1901), XIX, 89, XLVII, 193 (cited hereafter as *Jesuit Relations*).

13. Stearn and Stearn, *The Effect of Smallpox on the Destiny of the Amerindian, passim.* Among the specialized studies are Emily J. Blasingham, "The Depopulation of the Illinois Indians, Part 2, Conclusion," in *Ethnohistory*, III (1956), 361–412. Compare with Bert Anson, *The Miami Indians* (Norman: University of Oklahoma Press, 1970), p. 55.

14. Jacobs, *Dispossessing the American Indian: Indians and Whites on the Colonial Frontier*, pp. 31–40.

15. Incorporation was actively used by others, among them the Quapaw. Le Page du Pratz, *The History of Louisiana*, p. 303. Also, recruitment allowed the Fox tribe to rebound after warfare had reduced it from 50 to 60 individuals in 1726. William Jones, *Ethnography of the Fox Indians*, edited by Margaret W. Fisher (Bureau of American Ethnology, *Bulletin 125*, Washington, D.C., 1939), pp. 4–5. For a review of the ramifications of acculturation on population change see Steven Polgar, "Population History and Population Policy from an Anthropological Perspective," in *Current Anthropology*, XIII (1972), 203–11.

16. Eccles, *The Canadian Frontier, 1534–1760*, p. 128; also the Raudot memoir in W. Vernon Kinietz, *Indians of the Western Great Lakes, 1615–1760* (University of Michigan, Museum of Anthropology, *Occasional Contributions*, No. 10, Ann Arbor, 1940), pp. 341–410.

17. Griffin, "Eastern North American Archaeology: A Summary," in *Science*, CLVI, 175–91; for a description of the largest prehistoric aggregation at Cahokia in the American Bottom see Melvin L. Fowler, *Cahokia: Ancient Capital of the Midwest* (Addison-Wesley Module in Anthropology, 1974).

18. Harold Hickerson, "The Southwestern Chippewa, an Ethnohistorical Study," in American Anthropological Association *Memoir 92* (1962).

19. Illustrated by Gabriel Sagard, *The Long Journey to the Country of the Hurons*, edited by George M. Wrong (Toronto: Champlain Society, 1939), pp. 66–67; and again for the Illinois in *Jesuit Relations*, LIX, 127. Evidence of the same trading in advance of the French is recorded archaeologically in the Ohio River Valley where traders presumably did not travel. See Griffin, *The Fort Ancient Aspect*.

20. Harold Hickerson, "The Sociohistorical Significance of Two Chippewa Ceremonials," in *American Anthropologist*, LXV (1963), 67–85. Traditional aboriginal trade was most active between peoples commanding complementary resources. *Jesuit Relations*, XXXI, 209–11. For a review of aboriginal trade in the Great Lakes see Gary A. Wright, "Some Aspects of Early and Mid-Seventeenth Century Exchange Networks in the Western Great Lakes," in *Michigan Archaeologist*, XIII (1967), 181–97.

21. Noticed by Marquette (*Jesuit Relations*, LIX, 129) and others. At the Kaskaskia village watermelon seeds were found archaeologically. See Margaret K. Brown, *The Zimmerman Site, LaSalle County, Illinois* (Illinois State Museum, *Reports of Investigations*, 1975), in press. Botanical comments are to be found in Hugh C. Cutler and Thomas W. Whitaker, "History and Distribution of the Cultivated Curcurbits in the Americas," in *American Antiquity*, XXVI (1961), 484.

22. The following synopsis follows Eccles, *The Canadian Frontier, 1534–1760*, pp. 103–57.

23. *Ibid.*, p. 116.

24. *Ibid.*, p. 145.

25. *Ibid.*, p. 153.

26. Amply shown by Harold A. Innis, *The Fur Trade in Canada* (Rev. ed. New Haven: Yale University Press, 1962), Chapter II, pt. 5, especially pp. 110–11.

27. The history of both posts shows this development. See Walter Havighurst, *Three Flags at the Straits: The Forts of Mackinac* (Englewood Cliffs, N.J.: Prentice-Hall, 1966). See also Lewis R. Binford, "A Discussion of the Contrasts in the Development of the Settlement at Fort Michilimackinac under British and French Rule," in *Southeastern Archaeological Conference Newsletter*, IX (Lexington, Ky., 1961), 50–52.

28. See Philip Pittman, *The Present State of the European Settlements on the Mississippi* . . . (an exact reprint of the original London edition, 1770, edited by Frank H. Hodder [Cleveland: Arthur H. Clark Co., 1916]), p. 107; Anson, *The Miami Indians*. Note Pontiac's resentment of white settlement in Howard H. Peckham, *Pontiac and the Indian Uprising* (Princeton, N.J.: Princeton University Press, 1947), pp. 114–16.

29. Eccles, *The Canadian Frontier, 1534–1760*, p. 157.

30. Nelson V. Russell, *The British Regime in Michigan and the Old Northwest, 1760–1796* (Northfield, Minn.: Carleton College, 1939); Innis, *The Fur Trade in Canada*, pp. 166–68.

31. Innis, *The Fur Trade in Canada*, pp. 176–80.

32. Alexander Henry, *Travels and Adventures in Canada and the Indian Territories*, edited by James Bain (Rutland, Vt.: Charles E. Tuttle Co., 1969), pp. 183–84; Donald G. Creighton, *The Commercial Empire of the St. Lawrence, 1760–1850* (Toronto: Ryerson Press, 1937), pp. 7–24.

33. For discussion see Peckham, *Pontiac and the Indian Uprising*, pp. 101–103; Jacobs, *Dispossessing the American Indian: Indians and Whites on the Colonial Frontier*, pp. 75–82; and Wilbur R. Jacobs, *Diplomacy and Indian Gifts: Anglo-French Rivalry Along the Ohio and Northwest Frontiers, 1748–1763* (Stanford: Stanford University Press, 1950), pp. 180–85.

34. Jacobs, *Diplomacy and Indian Gifts*, pp. 12, 74–75.

35. Hoffman, "Ancient Tribes Revisited," in *Ethnohistory*, XIV, 1–46.

36. Louise P. Kellogg, *The French Régime in Wisconsin and the Northwest* (Madison: State Historical Society of Wisconsin, 1925), pp. 121–26. Note that the population clustered around Green Bay climbed to 20,000 (*Jesuit Relations*, LIX, 221). Later in 1683 the same number gathered around Fort St. Louis (Temple, *Indian Villages of the Illinois Country: Historic Tribes*, p. 27). For Detroit, see Peckham, *Pontiac and the Indian Uprising*, pp. 8–9.

37. Peckham, *Pontiac and the Indian Uprising*, pp. 8–9; Temple, *Indian Villages of the Illinois Country, Historic Tribes*, pp. 60, 86.

38. H. Clyde Wilson, "A New Interpretation of the Wild Rice District of Wisconsin," in *American Anthropologist*, LVIII (1956), 1060.

39. Peckham, *Pontiac and the Indian Uprising*, p. 9.

40. Anthony F. C. Wallace, *The Death and Rebirth of the Seneca* (New York: Alfred A. Knopf, 1970), pp. 112–14.

41. Perrot in Emma Helen Blair, *The Indian Tribes of the Upper Mississippi Valley* . . . (2 volumes. Cleveland: Arthur H. Clark Co., 1911), I, 146–203.

42. Ives Goddard, "Historical and Philological Evidence Regarding the Identification of the Mascouten," in *Ethnohistory*, XIX (1972), 123–34.

43. The Seneca appear to have been the most aggressive on the western frontier. They drove away the Wenro in 1638 and the Neutral in 1647. The latter had already driven away their neighbors the Erie about 1644. By the end of the decade

the League defeated the Huron confederacy (1649–50) and dispersed the Huron tribes. The Petun-Neutral were likewise evacuated from the new location in 1651. Recruitment by the League tribes was conspicuous in the 1650s, and by 1654 the Wenro, Erie, and the Anadasts were incorporated ethnically. Marian E. White, "Ethnic Identification and Iroquois Groups in Western New York and Ontario," in *Ethnohistory*, XVIII (1971), 19–20; Elisabeth Tooker, *An Ethnography of the Huron Indians, 1615–1649* (Bureau of American Ethnology, *Bulletin 190*, Washington, D.C., 1964), p. 17.

44. On the role of guns in breaking the middleman monopoly relationships, see Innis, *The Fur Trade in Canada*, p. 54. The incursion of the Iroquois into the Illinois country dates as early as 1655. See George T. Hunt, *The Wars of the Iroquois* (Madison: University of Wisconsin Press, 1940), pp. 145–46.

45. Wallace, *The Death and Rebirth of the Seneca*, p. 113.

46. *Ibid.*, p. 114.

47. Hickerson, "The Southwestern Chippewa, an Ethnohistorical Study," in American Anthropological Association *Memoir 92*, pp. 65–72, 78–81.

48. *Ibid.*, pp. 65–72; Harold Hickerson, *The Chippewa and their Neighbors: A Study in Ethnohistory (Studies in Anthropological Method*. New York: Holt, Rinehart & Winston, 1970), pp. 37–50.

49. See Hickerson, *The Chippewa and their Neighbors: A Study in Ethnohistory*, p. 45.

50. For a detailed review of Central Algonkian social organization, see Charles Callender, *Social Organization of the Central Algonkian Indians* (Milwaukee Public Museum, *Publications in Anthropology*, No. 7, 1962). For the warfare-oriented basis of patrilineal clan organization see also George P. Murdock, "North American Social Organization," in *Davidson Journal of Anthropology*, I (1955), 88–89. The general model for the adaptive context for such forms of segmentary kinship systems has been developed by Marshall B. Sahlins, "The Segmentary Lineage: An Organization of Predatory Expansion," in *American Anthropologist*, LXIII (1961), 322–45.

51. Nancy O. Lurie, "Winnebago Protohistory," in *Culture and History: Essays in Honor of Paul Radin*, edited by Stanley Diamond (New York: Columbia University Press, 1960), pp. 790–808.

52. Callender, *Social Organization of the Central Algonkian Indians*; Blasingham, "The Depopulation of the Illinois Indians, Part 2, Conclusion," in *Ethnohistory*, III, 361–412; Margaret K. Brown, "Cultural Transformation among the Illinois" (Ph.D. dissertation, Michigan State University, 1973).

53. Wallace, *The Death and Rebirth of the Seneca*, p. 195.

54. Tooker, *An Ethnography of the Huron Indians, 1615–1649*, p. 17; Trigger, *The Huron Farmers of the North*, pp. 76–78.

55. Wallace, *The Death and Rebirth of the Seneca*, pp. 39–43.

56. *Ibid.*, pp. 44–48.

57. The histories of mixed population have scarcely been handled. The largest populations presumably resided around missions where Jesuits and records make mention. See Gibault in Clarence W. Alvord and Clarence E. Carter, *Trade and Politics, 1767–1769 (Illinois Historical Collections*, XVI, Springfield, 1921), pp. 554–55; Natalia M. Belting, *Kaskaskia under the French Regime (Illinois Studies in the Social Sciences*, XXIX, No. 3, Urbana: University of Illinois Press, 1948); also Anson, *The Miami Indians*, pp. 55–56.

58. Charles E. Hunter, "The Delaware Nativist Revival of the Mid-Eighteenth Century," in *Ethnohistory*, XVIII (1971), 39–49.

59. Wallace, *The Death and Rebirth of the Seneca*, pp. 117–21.

60. Hickerson, "The Sociohistorical Significance of Two Chippewa Cere-

monials," in *American Anthropologist*, LXV, 67–85, and *The Chippewa and their Neighbors: A Study in Ethnohistory*.

61. Hickerson, *The Chippewa and their Neighbors: A Study in Ethnohistory*, pp. 59–61. An equally early historical reference to the ceremony is from the Illinois in their aggregated village on Lake Peoria. See Deliette in Theodore C. Pease and Raymond C. Werner, *The French Foundations* (*Illinois Historical Collections*, XXIII, Springfield, 1934), pp. 368–71. The ceremony is noted in another large aggregated settlement at Detroit. See Memoir of Sabrevois de Bleury in *The French Regime in Wisconsin, 1634–1727*, edited by Reuben Gold Thwaites (*Wisconsin Historical Collections*, XVI, Madison, 1902), p. 367.

62. The Huron assumed and maintained this middleman role until their dispersal; the Ottawa were next in the Great Lakes to block access to the Sioux and other tribes (Blair, *The Indian Tribes of the Upper Mississippi Valley*, I, 366). Later the Potawatomi blocked access to the Mascouten (*ibid.*, I, 322) and lastly the Fox blocked the route to the Dakota Sioux (Louise P. Kellogg [ed.], *Early Narratives of the Northwest, 1634–1699* [New York: Charles Scribner's Sons, 1917], p. 344). Most middleman tribes monopolized access via occupation of a coastline, but the Fox held a critical watershed. See James Silverberg, "The Kickapoo Indians: First One Hundred Years of White Contact in Wisconsin," in *Wisconsin Archaeologist*, XXXVIII (1957), 61–181. Best current overview of the phases of fur trade involvement is George I. Quimby, *Indian Culture and European Trade Goods: The Archaeology of the Historic Period in the Western Great Lakes Region* (Madison: University of Wisconsin Press, 1966). The geography of power has been applied to the Iroquois situation respecting European powers in the historic period. See Allen W. Trelease, "The Iroquois and the Western Fur Trade, a Problem in Interpretation," in *Mississippi Valley Historical Review*, XLIX (1962), 32–51.

63. For example, Green Bay in the 1680s (Reuben Gold Thwaites [ed.], *Lahontan's New Voyages to North America* [2 volumes. Chicago: A. C. McClurg & Co., 1905], I, 168), and Detroit in 1714 (O'Callaghan [ed.], *Documents Relative to the Colonial History of New York*, IX, 866).

64. Mary W. Herman, "The Social Aspect of Huron Property," in *American Anthropologist*, LVIII (1956), 1044–58; *Jesuit Relations*, X, 303.

65. Jacobs, *Diplomacy and Indian Gifts, passim*.

66. For an authoritative overview see Griffin, "Eastern North American Archaeology: A Summary," in *Science*, CLVI, 175–91.

67. J. N. B. Hewitt, "Calumet," in *Handbook of American Indians North of Mexico*, edited by Frederick W. Hodge (2 parts. Bureau of American Ethnology, *Bulletin 30*, Washington, D.C., 1910), pt. 1, pp. 191–95.

68. The ceremony was known by 1667 (Blair, *The Indian Tribes of the Upper Mississippi Valley*, I, 350) and presumably was not current at the time of Nicolet's visit to the Winnebago in 1634 when another greeting ceremony was used (Lurie, "Winnebago Protohistory," in *Culture and History: Essays in Honor of Paul Radin*, p. 800). Its distribution is summarized by William N. Fenton in *The Iroquois Eagle Dance. An Offshoot of the Calumet Dance* (Bureau of American Ethnology, *Bulletin 156*, Washington, D.C., 1953), pp. 172–206. The regional distribution of the dance as a means of cementing intertribal relationships was succinctly observed by Charlevoix in 1721 (Pierre Charlevoix, *Journal of a Voyage to North America*, edited by Louise P. Kellogg [2 volumes. Chicago: Caxton Club, 1923], I, 304) and again by Joseph F. Lafitau, *Moeurs des Sauvages Ameriquains . . .* (2 volumes. Paris: Saugrain l'aîné, 1724), II, 314.

69. Fenton, *The Iroquois Eagle Dance, An Offshoot of the Calumet Dance*, pp. 163–64.

Spanish Indian Policy and the Struggle for Empire in the Southeast, 1513-1776

JOHN J. TEPASKE

For the English, French, and Spaniards in the New World, many factors determined their success or failure in the struggle for empire. Geography, timing, natural resources, climate, leadership, technology, availability of a trained soldiery, material support, migration, myths, and values all played an important role in the European conquest of America. Equally important were the native societies encountered by the Europeans—the size of the Indian populations and their economic, social, political, and religious institutions. The Spaniards, for example, unlike either the English or French, faced large, densely populated Indian civilizations with complex institutions, particularly those of the Aztec, Maya, and Inca. Central Mexico, in fact, had an indigenous population estimated at twenty-five million at the time of the conquest in 1519.[1] This was crucial in determining the direction of conquest and later in shaping Spanish colonial institutions. Such practices as the *encomienda*,[2] *mita* and *repartimiento*,[3] reduction,[4] mission, and tribute exaction all reflected Spanish methods for organizing, controlling, and exploiting large Indian populations with a high degree of civilization.

Elsewhere in the Spanish empire, however, this was not the case. On the Chilean frontier, in the Río de la Plata region, and in the American Southwest, the Spaniards encountered scattered groups of Indians, thinly populated, with relatively simple social and economic organization. In these areas the early conquistadores and their successors fashioned a vastly different Indian policy in response both to local conditions and to the Indian societies they faced. This was also true in the American Southeast, the area now encompassed by Florida, Georgia, and Alabama. How the Spaniards dealt with the Indians in the Southeast, the place of

John J. TePaske, a specialist in Spanish colonial history, is Professor of History, Duke University.

the natives in the imperial struggle in this area, and the effect of this struggle on Indian culture are the themes of this paper.

First Encounters: The Shaping of Spanish Indian Policy in the Southeast, 1513–1565

Spanish incursions into the Southeast in the first half of the sixteenth century were sporadic, not relentless and persistent like the Spanish conquest of Mexico and Peru. Juan Ponce de León made the first penetration of Florida in 1513 and established basic patterns for Spanish-Indian relations for the next half century, a pattern of force and violence to subjugate the Indians and bring them under Spanish domination. This was implicit in Ponce's initial patent of February 23, 1512, which gave him the right to explore and settle Florida, to pacify the Indians by force, to take Indian slaves, and to allot these slaves to his soldiers.[5] When he arrived in Florida, therefore, he followed the terms of his patent. The Indians, however, resisted fiercely. Particularly active in the Charlotte Harbor-Tampa Bay areas, favorite landing sites for later expeditions, Ponce could take no Indian slaves and ultimately had to withdraw to Puerto Rico to plan a new expedition. Meanwhile, the Indians had been introduced to the ways of the white man.

On his second expedition in 1521 Ponce was bound by many more restrictions in his dealings with the natives. He could no longer take slaves, except those who refused to make their obeisance to the King of Castile and to the Catholic faith. In Spain jurists had drawn up a document (the *requerimiento*) to be read to the natives before the Spanish conquistadores initiated hostilities against them. The *requerimiento* demanded two things of the Indians: (1) they had to promise obedience to the King of Spain and the pope and (2) allow the Catholic faith to be preached to them. Refusal to bow to these demands meant the Indians could be taken as slaves.[6] Interpreted to the Indians only if an interpreter was available, the document may seem farcical by modern standards, but in the early sixteenth century, it established the basis for a just war and helped salve the consciences of Spanish policy makers.

The new restrictions binding Ponce de León made no difference in his dealings with the Indians. Again it was the musket, sword, lance, horse, and dog of the Spaniard against the bow and arrow, spear, dart, and club of the Indians. Again the Indians were intransigently hostile and difficult to subdue. They had come to expect violence from the white man and that is what they gave him in return. Again Ponce took no slaves, ultimately being forced to return to Puerto Rico, the victim of an Indian arrow which had pierced his side. And those who followed were no more successful. Pánfilo de Narváez in 1528; Hernando de

Soto in 1539; and Tristán de Luna y Arellano in 1559 all tried to conquer the Indians by force. All failed.[7]

Fray Luis Cancer de Barbastro was the one exception to these efforts to subjugate the Indians by force of arms. In 1549 this Dominican disciple of the defender of the Indians, Bartolomé de las Casas, determined to make a spiritual conquest by peaceful means alone to prove that peace and good will were more powerful weapons than muskets and swords in winning over the natives. Unfortunately, perhaps, he chose the Gulf Coast as the site for his effort at peaceful conversion and subjugation. Conditioned to view the white man as a man of violence rather than a man of peace, the Indians ultimately turned on Cancer and his compatriots in the same way they had turned on Ponce de León earlier. In the end they clubbed the idealistic Dominican to death in full view of his brethren lining the deck of a Spanish ship safely floating in the bay.[8]

These early efforts at both forceful and peaceful domination of Florida and the Southeast all failed. The Indians were hostile, and there were no mines like those of Potosí or Zacatecas for the Spaniards to exploit. Sporadic efforts to explore and settle the Southeast had been a terrible waste of lives and money for both the Crown and the individuals who financed the expeditions into the area. Thus, in September, 1561, Philip II ordered the abandonment of all attempts to explore and settle Florida; it had proved to be nothing but a drain on the resources of Spain.[9]

While the formative period of Spanish-Indian relationships in the Southeast may have been characterized primarily by violent confrontation, the Spaniard seems to have had a peculiar ambivalence about the Indian. On the one side, even the most hard-bitten soldier of fortune was fascinated by the seeming simplicity, goodness, and innocence of the natives. They were in many ways the pristine children of nature, unspoiled, truly the noble savages. "They invite you to share anything that they possess, and show as much love as if their hearts went with it," wrote Columbus. Or Peter Martyr: "They seem to live in that golden world, of the which old writers speak so much, wherein men lived simply and innocently without enforcement of laws, without quarreling, judges and libels, content only to satisfy nature."[10] Father Cancer exemplified this view and tried to show that it was unnecessary to use force to bring these innocent people under Spanish tutelage. Many of the early conquistadores in the Southeast held the same opinion. But on the other side they also believed the Indians could be cunning, deceitful, cruel, and barbaric and came to this view with good reason. Ponce de León, Narváez, de Soto, and de Luna were in a struggle for survival. They could not survive in Florida without food from the Indians to sustain them. Thus, the Spaniard not only conquered the Indian by force of arms, but he also despoiled him of his food supply, the dried meat and dried fish and the corn and beans which the Indian had set aside for his own use. With different diet patterns—it is estimated that the Spaniard ate twenty times as much as the Indian—it was not uncommon for a Spanish band in the Southeast to devour a village's winter supply of food in a few days. Why the Indians took arms against the Spaniards or lied to get rid of them seems clear enough. If the Spaniards were not defeated in battle or driven off by other means, the Indians themselves could not survive. One favorite ploy for the Indians was to describe the rich mines and golden cities far away over the next mountain range or across the next river, a wealth of riches to be found only if the Spaniard would move farther on.[11] When the conquistadores failed to find these illusory cities, they oftentimes took revenge on the deceitful liars who had described them in the first place. Whether the Indian was a noble savage is moot, of course, but there is no question that the Spanish intrusion forced him to lose whatever innocence he might have had before the white man came.

Spanish Indian Policy and the Extension of Empire, 1562–1670

Within a year Philip II had to change his mind about settling Florida. French encroachment upon the area in 1562 represented a clear challenge to Spanish ships plying the Bahama Channel, and Philip decided to drive out the interlopers in what became the first imperial clash in the Southeast. In September, 1565, Pedro Menéndez de Avilés led a Spanish expedition against the French, destroyed Fort Caroline on the Saint John's River, massacred another body of men at Matanzas Point south of present-day Saint Augustine, and established the first permanent settlement in Florida to assure the Spanish hold on the area.[12]

From 1565 Florida took on strategic importance as a protection for the treasure fleets but in reality was a flimsily defended backwash. Saint Augustine was the focal point of Spanish power—if it can be called that —and later the erection of small forts at Apalache near present-day Tallahassee and at Pensacola shored up the defenses of the colony, but these were only tiny outposts. Until 1670 the single most important factor in maintaining imperial control over the Southeast was the Franciscan mission. If Spain had claimed the area initially by virtue of papal donation or prior discovery and exploration, the missions provided an opportunity for cementing this claim by effective occupation. If the utopian aims of the Jesuits and Franciscans could be fused with the imperial goals of the Crown, so much the better for Spain and the Church.

The mission story has been well told elsewhere, but briefly, the Jesuits were the first in the field after the founding of Saint Augustine in 1565. The followers of Ignatius Loyola extended their efforts as far north as the Potomac River and south to present-day Miami and Tampa. The Jesuits labored diligently among the Indians but found them hard to subdue by peaceful means. After a number of revolts and the macabre martyrdom of a number of their order, they left Florida in 1572.[13] Immediately the Franciscans filled the gap, and over the next century developed a flourishing mission system in three areas—Apalache (present-day western Florida, southern Georgia, and Alabama), Guale (coastal Georgia), and Timucua (north-central Florida). At their peak the Franciscans established at least thirty missions in these three districts with over fifty missionaries serving more than 13,000 baptized Indians.[14]

The missions proved an effective way of making a peaceful conquest of the area and securing imperial control at little cost to the Crown. The Franciscan policy in Florida and the Southeast was peaceful persuasion. Unlike the Franciscans in the Southwest, they established their missions *without* the support of Spanish soldiers. Using small gifts and their proficiency with the Indian languages to establish their credibility, the missionaries usually picked the village of the regional chief to teach, preach, and baptize. They expanded their efforts into other pueblos, establishing new missions as the population and number of conversions warranted. The Franciscans had two goals—converting the Indians to Christianity and bringing them at least some benefits of Hispanic civilization, particularly instruction in more efficient agricultural techniques. In their work among the Indians they were remarkably tolerant, even to the point of countenancing the Indians' cannibalism.[15]

Although the Franciscans did not impose a rigorous regimen on the Indians of the Southeast, they did make some demands on them. The Indians had to provide the friars with a wooden log every time they came to Mass and with eggs and other food at Christmas and on saints' days. They were required to adorn their huts with crucifixes, religious ornaments, and other manifestations of their religiosity. They had to take instruction from the Franciscans in catechism and Spanish. At times they were used as forced laborers, either in the mission itself or in Saint Augustine. The Franciscans also tried to put a stop to war dances, consensual marriages, and religious practices which ran counter to Roman Catholic rituals or beliefs and regulated the movement of the Indians into Saint Augustine. No native could enter without obtaining prior permission from the governor.[16]

On balance the Franciscans were humane, dedicated models of the Christian faith they preached and taught. With some exceptions they did *not* extort exorbitant amounts of tribute, labor, or wealth from the

Indians as some of their brethren did in Peru and Mexico. Until the eighteenth century, when their lives were no longer safe on the frontier, they chose *not* to reside comfortably in their monastery in Saint Augustine to be served by the Indians they had proselyted; rather, the Franciscans labored among the Indians, teaching, preaching, and assisting them with their planting. Also, when contrasted with English practices later, it is important to remember what else the Franciscans did *not* do. They did *not* furnish the Indians with rum and wine. They did *not* give them firearms. They did *not* take Indian slaves. They did *not* despoil the Indians of their land. They did *not* turn one tribe or village against another.

Finally, Franciscan activities among the Indians did not fundamentally transform Indian communities—social structure, economic patterns, diet, technology, and the like. The Indians retained their decentralized pattern of local autonomy. They continued to eat corn, pumpkins, beans, game, and fish and to wear the same clothing, the crude skins and rough tunics they fashioned themselves. Although the bishop of Cuba in 1674 counted 4,081 women walking about naked from the waist up and suggested that they use moss to cover this part of their anatomy, patterns of dress were otherwise not altered. The Indians' principal weapons continued to be the bow and arrow and stone axe, and they continued to make their way on foot, not on horseback. Their crude huts with their bearskin roofs remained unchanged. In other words the Indians were little affected by the Spanish presence.

For Spain extending and holding the empire by a chain of missions was an ideal policy. The good friars did not cost much, yet they insured the Crown a stronghold on the frontier. For the tiny Spanish garrisons in Saint Augustine and Apalache, the Indian communities were a source of food. To be sure the Florida missions were no utopia; periodic revolts and martyrdom of some Franciscans testify to Indian dissatisfaction under Franciscan tutelage. Yet the Franciscans did not destroy the integrity of Indian communities, take slaves, make self-reliant Indians into creatures dependent upon rum and European goods, destroy native handicrafts, or turn tribe against tribe.

COMPETITION FOR EMPIRE IN THE SOUTHEAST: THE DECLINE OF SPANISH POWER AND INDIAN POLICY, 1670–1732

The halcyon days for Spain and the Franciscans ended abruptly in 1670 with the founding of English Carolina. Prior to 1670 the Spaniards —and the Franciscans—were left to their own devices, unchallenged and uninhibited. The English in Virginia posed no threat, and there was virtually no contact between the English and Spanish along the Atlantic seaboard. The only danger to the Spanish foothold in Florida came from an occasional raid by pirates or privateers, like that of Sir Francis Drake in 1585, or from an Indian revolt, but these were usually quelled easily. In other words, for a little over a century Spanish imperial claims on the Southeast went uncontested.

The founding of Carolina broke the Spanish monopoly on the Southeast and, more specifically, over the Indians. From the outset English Indian traders began to intrude on areas hitherto the exclusive province of the Spanish Franciscans. And they came like Henry Woodward in 1685 with rum, guns, cloth, powder, shot, tools, and a host of other goods which they offered to the Indians on favorable terms for their deer- and bearskins.[17] If the friars were the Spanish vanguard among the natives in the late sixteenth century, traders like Woodward served the same purpose for the English in the late seventeenth. How did these traders influence imperial relationships? First, their rum and guns easily won over the Indians to English alliances. Acquiring very quickly a taste for strong drink and seeing the advantages of muskets for hunting and fighting, Upper and Lower Creeks, Yamasees, Guales, and others flocked to the English banner and forced the rapid contraction of the Franciscan mission frontier. In 1680 warriors loyal to the English raided the Spanish mission on Jekyll Island. Four years later hordes of Guales along the Georgia coast turned against their Franciscan benefactors after being flooded with material favors by English traders. In 1685, in fact, English Indians made incursions deep into the Timucua mission district in north-central Florida, raiding and burning the mission at Santa Catalina. As a result of these attacks, in 1686, sixteen years after the founding of Carolina, the Franciscans were forced to retreat south of the Saint Mary's River. At the same time in the interior of Lower Creek country Henry Woodward was active in urging his newly won allies to make raids on the Apalache missions near present-day Tallahassee.[18] Thus during the thirty years from 1670 to 1700, the extensive Franciscan mission system of thirty missions scattered throughout the Southeast was in shambles, reduced to a few towns of Christian Indians near Fort San Luis de Apalache and Saint Augustine and to those along the coast south of the Saint Mary's River.

Queen Anne's War (1702–1713) was the *coup de grace* for the Franciscans. In 1702 the Carolinians swept into Florida with their Indian allies and destroyed all the missions in the Saint Augustine area except those under the cannon of Fort San Marcos.[19] Two years later Governor James Moore and a large band of Upper Creeks ravaged Apalache and the Christian Indian villages still remaining there. Taking large numbers of slaves, Moore and his band gave no quarter. According to one Spanish account, the English and their Indians devised "exquisite methods of torture" using hot knives to kill Apalache prisoners. Others they tore limb from limb. "Like hungry wolves," he states, they butchered the Christian Indians until "the grass turned scarlet with the blood of these poor people." In the end this raid ended all mission activity in Apalache and forced the evacuation of Fort San Luis.[20] And things got worse as the conflict wore on. By 1711 only 401 Indians still remained loyal to the Spaniards, and they were living in villages close to Saint Augustine.[21] By 1713 when the war ended, it seemed clear that the Spanish hold on Florida was in grave danger.

Clearly the Indians were a key factor in the British success against the Spaniards. They had proven to be useful, effective allies during the war, and prospects seemed good that they would continue to serve their English compatriots as agents of imperial expansion. The Spaniards simply had no way of competing with English traders and seemed doomed in Florida. But two elements served to right the balance of power in the Southeast and lessen English influence among the Indians. First, the French became active in the Indian trade after the founding of Mobile in 1701 and keen competitors with the English for the loyalty of the Indians. At the same time this new competition exposed a great many abuses of the English monopoly—cheating on weights and measures, beating Indian debtors, seizing relatives of debtors as slaves in payment of what was owed, charging exorbitant prices, and repossessing goods for nonpayment of debts.[22] Moreover, the English traders had encouraged intertribal warfare, paying Indians in rum and guns for slaves they took. These slaves, in turn, were sent to Barbados or sold to rice or indigo planters on the coast.[23]

These abuses culminated in the Yamasee revolt of April, 1715. Angered over their mistreatment by English traders, Yamasees and Creeks attacked English settlements throughout Carolina and almost took Charleston. (Had it not been for Cherokee support of the English, the town might have fallen to the rebels.) In the end, the Carolinians repelled the Yamasee and Creek assaults but not before the revolt had opened a new epoch in the imperial struggle in the Southeast. After 1715 the English lost their monopoly on the Indian trade and Indian alliances and had to compete with the French and, to a lesser extent, the Spanish. Also with the French now engaged in the Indian trade, some tribes soon came to realize the advantages of shifting alliances, of playing off one European nation against another to get the rum, wine, powder, shot, and tools they needed. Others decided on a neutrality policy in an attempt to get the European traders to vie for their alliances. Old Brims, emperor of the Lower Creek confederation, was particularly a master at such a policy.[24]

The Spaniards also entered the competition for Indian alliances and attempted to win their loyalty through favorable trading terms, but they were at a considerable disadvantage. They had no large corps of Indian traders like Henry Woodward, Thomas Nairne, Thomas Welch, Theophilus Hastings, or John Musgrove to deal with the Indians. They were further handicapped by the meager supplies at their disposal to trade with the Indians. Florida was a poor colony which depended upon a subsidy from Mexico for its survival. Even the Spanish regulars serving at Fort San Marcos in Saint Augustine were not regularly paid or supplied with full rations. Providing goods and supplies to the Indians meant depriving the garrison and the Spanish residents of Saint Augustine of their basic needs. Still, particularly between 1715 and 1723 when the Florida governor did his best to woo the Indians with gifts and favors, he was successful among the Lower Creeks, rebuilt the fort at Apalache, and dispatched Spanish emissaries to obtain temporary treaties with the Creeks.[25]

THE INDIANS AND THE FOUNDING OF GEORGIA: THE SHIFT IN THE BALANCE OF POWER IN THE SOUTHEAST, 1733–1776

The pattern of shifting alliances and competition for the Indian tribes in the Southeast after the Yamasee revolt ended with the founding of Georgia by James Oglethorpe in 1733. This energetic leader embarked on a vigorous policy of courting the Indians, particularly the Lower Creeks. Like the Carolinians before him he used traders and favorable trade terms to woo the Indians. Crucial at the outset were the activities of Johnny and Mary Musgrove, who led the way as Henry Woodward had in Carolina earlier. Johnny was an Indian trader; Mary was his Indian wife, but more important, the niece of the Lower Creek emperor, Brims. Both were instrumental in establishing Oglethorpe's alliances with the Lower Creeks that brought them once again into the English orbit.[26] Also crucial was Oglethorpe's use of personal diplomacy and his willingness to endure the hardships of travel into the interior to dicker with the Indians. Moreover, in 1734 he personally escorted the Lower Creek chief, Tomochichi, and a party of warriors to England, where they were feted grandly and brought before George II to make mutual professions of everlasting friendship.[27] For all these efforts Oglethorpe got a large land cession, defensive alliances, and the right to settle but not claim certain unoccupied Indian lands; in return he promised trade and protection to the Indians.

This rash of activity served to dissipate Spanish influence among the Lower Creeks and gave Oglethorpe the upper hand. As usual, after 1734 the pragmatic, well-supplied English began courting Indian allies as war drew nearer. Oglethorpe, for example, personally journeyed into the Lower Creek country in 1739 to meet with a grand council of 7,000 Creeks, Coosee, Talapusa, Choctaw, and Chickasaw warriors and got promises of alliances.[28] When the War of Jenkins' Ear broke out later in the year, he used the same Indians first in cutting the main road between Saint Augustine and Apalache. Soon after, his bands of Lower Creeks attacked the two Spanish outposts of Pupo and Picolata, protecting the Saint John's River and the western flank of Saint Augustine. In the end this raid turned into a rout when the Spanish garrisons stationed at the two blockhouses fled.[29] Later, in the summer of 1740, Indian scouts and raiders served Oglethorpe in the unsuccessful siege of Saint Augustine,[30] while in 1742 the Georgia governor gave the same Indians the credit for aiding in the ambush and defeat of the Spanish force attempting to take Fort Frederica.[31]

A nagging question remains to be answered: if Oglethorpe had the overwhelming support of the Indians, if he had a military alliance with seven thousand Indians, why could he not drive out the Spaniards? The fact was that the Indians were grossly unreliable allies. In 1741, for example, Oglethorpe wrote to the Duke of Newcastle that the only way he could get the Indians to fight was to offer them presents, and, even then, they could not be counted on to keep their promises.[32] To demonstrate the kind of problem Oglethorpe and the other European powers faced in the Southeast, one can look at his experience in March, 1743, in attempting to use Indians to assault Saint Augustine. As background, late in 1742 a group of Spanish-inspired Yamasees had destroyed the English trading post at Mount Venture on the Altamaha River, a favorite site for the Lower Creeks to exchange their deer- and bearskins for English goods.[33] Anxious to get revenge on the Spaniards and the Yamasee, eighty Creek warriors under Chigilly joined Oglethorpe and his regulars in the retaliatory raid organized in March, 1743. On March 9 Chigilly's band moved toward Saint Augustine from Oglethorpe's base camp on the Saint John's River and ambushed a Spanish longboat on the Diego River near Fort San Marcos, killing a Spanish soldier and five forced laborers and wounding eighteen others. Returning to the banks of the Saint John's on March 11, the Indians presented Oglethorpe with five scalps, a severed hand, and a number of severed arms, boasting they had killed over forty Spaniards in all. Oglethorpe ordered wine and food as a victory celebration. After plying the Indians with drink, he then asked their support for an all-out attack on Saint Augustine. The Indians flatly refused, and all but four left the English camp to return to their villages in the interior.[34] This was characteristic of the dependability of the Indians as allies. Not only Oglethorpe and his successors in Georgia but also the French and Spanish had the same problem in securing permanent alliances with the natives. That the Indians were unreliable was a hard lesson that all the European powers came to learn in the struggle for empire in the Southeast.

The failure of the Spanish attack on Frederica in 1742 and of Oglethorpe's raid on Saint Augustine in 1743 marked the establishment of an uncomfortable equilibrium in the Southeast. The Indians were in some measure responsible for this change. They had learned the disadvantages of allying too firmly with one European power against another and courted first one side and then the other in the quest for rum, guns, and tools. When the Spaniards set up a new trading post in Apalache in 1745, for example, a flood of Indians stripped the store of all its supplies, leaving the agent there forlorn over his empty shelves and his failure to get any promises from the Indians. That the Spaniards had any goods at all to establish a trading post was something of a change, but the Indians were quick to seize the opportunity to acquire whatever supplies were for sale in Apalache. Still another factor in maintaining this equilibrium was the increasing number of intertribal wars. As the Indians acquired guns, as they became temporary allies of either one European or another, they found themselves fighting their fellow Indians. Intertribal animosities had existed before the arrival of the Europeans, but the use of Indians as allies in the imperial struggle in the Southeast sharply increased their differences. Thus, the Indians oftentimes spent as much time fighting each other as they did fighting the English, French, and Spaniards. And the Creek-Cherokee War of 1750–1752 was a good example of the kind of internecine warfare that neutralized the effectiveness of the Indians as pawns in the imperial struggle. Still another factor, which cannot be documented but which seems apparent, is the demographic decline of the Indians. They simply were not available in as great a number as they were in the late seventeenth century and early eighteenth.[35]

The peaceful transfer of Florida to English control in 1764 ended the three-cornered struggle for empire in the Southeast. English authority was unchallenged, and for the Spaniards imperial concerns shifted to the Mississippi Valley. Here they encountered the same kind of challenges from English traders that they had faced in the Southeast, but supply lines were much longer and the English could not furnish the Indians the quantity of goods required to make them allies. The Spaniards in the Mississippi Valley genuinely feared these English intrusions as the first step in an effort aimed at the heart of the Spanish empire in New Spain and the wealth of its mines, but that is the subject for new investigation and outside the scope of this paper.[36]

THE IMPERIAL STRUGGLE IN THE SOUTHEAST AND THE EFFECT ON THE INDIANS: SOME BRIEF OBSERVATIONS

The coming of the white man had many effects on the Indians of the Southeast, as they became embroiled in the imperial struggle that ensued after 1670. As has already been pointed out, the Franciscans came early, in the 1570s, to intrude on the religious lives of the Indians and to try to bring them a few advantages of Hispanic civilization. For the most part, however, they wrought no basic transformation in Indian society—diet, dress, social and political structure, and the like. The appearance of the English and the French, however, had far greater influence, far greater impact than the presence of the Spanish missionaries. First, and perhaps most important, the Indian trade established by the English and the French created a taste for European goods among the Indians of the Southeast and made them completely dependent upon it. This, in turn, had a number of ramifications. According to one observer, Indian expertise in the manual arts declined when they began to use superior European tools and implements. Not only did they lose their talents in handicrafts—weaving, making of bows, arrows, axes, seeding sticks, and the like—but they also became so covetous of European goods that they would go to any lengths to procure them.[37] This meant a sharp increase in intertribal warfare for the purpose of taking slaves. Slaves, the Indians found, could be sold to English merchants for rum, guns, powder, shot, and cloth. The English in turn could sell the Indian slaves for profit to plantation owners along the coast of South Carolina or in Barbados. In fact in 1708 Indian slaves made up 14 per cent of the population of South Carolina.[38]

The introduction of rum, brandy, and wine also had a real effect on the Indians. Prior to the introduction of strong drink by the Europeans, the Indians apparently had no comparable beverage available for ceremonial or psychological uses. The Spaniards had strictly prohibited distribution of wine or brandy, but with the coming of the English rum trade the Indians soon became prolific users. The English, in particular, were expert at plying the Indians with strong drink and then extracting favorable trade terms from them, getting them to sell or exchange their skins for little or nothing. As noted, this was one of the causes of the Yamasee War. Unlike the Spaniards or the French, the English also obtained generous land cessions from the Indians, oftentimes after lengthy bouts of drinking. Perhaps, though, the Indian addiction to strong drink has been too greatly exaggerated. If they drank a great deal, so did the white men they dealt with. And they both drank for the same reasons—on ritual occasions and holidays or at certain times temporarily to break down the formal social norms and barriers that structured their lives, much in the same way drinking patterns are used in contemporary society by a variety of cultures and peoples. To picture the Indian as a drunkard completely at the mercy of the unscrupulous white man hardly reflects the reality of the situation.

From a comparative point of view, however, the English used liquor far more than the Spaniards and French to gain Indian allies and had much less compunction about its distribution among the natives. The Spaniards, we know, prohibited trade in wine or brandy, at least until the English came to the Southeast and forced them to compete for the Indians in the rum and gun trade. The French, it appears, at least tried to *control* the liquor trade. Actually, the question of accountability of the Indian while under the influence of liquor was a serious one for the French, who recognized the Indian as independent and free to live under his own laws. Thus if an Indian committed a crime while under the influence of liquor, was he accountable for his actions and to whom? After all the French introduced the liquor in the first place. In 1664, for example, when an Algonkian Indian under the influence of strong drink raped the wife of a French settler, the question arose whether or not he could be prosecuted by French authorities. The final decision was to let each individual Indian tribe control its own members. In 1714 the problem arose again when the Indians declared that the French had no right to jail them for drunkenness because they were free and independent, not subject to French law. The Indians argued that those who provided the liquor were the real offenders for whatever crime was perpetrated while the Indians drank. To their credit, the French agreed to the Indian arguments and attempted to control the liquor trade and to prosecute illegal suppliers for those offenses committed by the Indian imbibing illegal beverages.[39]

The English also introduced firearms to the Indians, forcing other drastic changes in their cultural and social patterns. Firearms enabled the Indians to hunt more easily and to make war more effectively. Guns could be used for killing game and against other tribes to take slaves to trade with the English for liquor, shot, guns, powder, and other supplies. The Indians could use firearms also to war on European settlements, on their own or inspired by a rival European power. Muskets slowly came to replace the bow and arrow as a method for hunting and warfare, and in Indian society the marksman came to have higher status than the expert bowman. Whether the musket was crucial in breaking the ecological balance in the Southeast is open to question, but it may have been one factor in the decline of the Indian population in the eighteenth century. Also, control over the trade in firearms was a way in which the English held sway over certain chiefs. Giving these chiefs the right to sell or exchange guns in return for their allegiance was an effective policy for the English. Fittingly, one of the best-known Indian chiefs among the Lower Creeks in the 1750s had the name, "Gun Merchant."

Still another effect of the intrusion of the Europeans was the alteration in the political structure of the tribes, particularly the Lower Creeks. Until the coming of the white man the Lower Creeks were a loose confederation of independent villages, each with its own chief and body of ruling elders. Succession to the chief's post was matrilineal. Over all the villages of the confederation was an emperor, whose influence depended upon his wisdom, charisma, and moral suasion. Otherwise, he had no real power; the chief of each village could go his own way, one important reason for the myriad shifts in Indian alliances over the eighteenth century. But Europeans—French, Spaniards, and English alike—did not find it easy to work within such a system. All were used to dealing within a patrilineal framework with the eldest son of the chief falling heir to his father's office. In addition all three powers could see the advantages to be gained in establishing a more centralized political structure among the Indians. Securing the allegiance of only one chief holding sway over a number of tribes was far easier than having to win over the *mico* of each village. In subtle ways, therefore, the political structure of the natives slowly gave way to a patrilineal, more European structure.[40]

In sum, these are just a few of the observations which came from comparative study of European Indian policy in the Southeast. When one juxtaposes the relatively humane policy of missionization and Christianization pursued by the Spanish and the English practice of wooing the Indians with material goods, he can, perhaps, say with some certainty that the offer of material rewards was far more effective than spiritual rewards in winning over the Indians. But at the same time that rum and guns proved effective in obtaining Indian allies in the imperial struggle in the Southeast, these same goods had a disastrous effect on the Indians, transforming their social, economic, cultural and political norms, and leading eventually to their domination by the white man. In the Southeast, the English prevailed, and if we can draw moral lessons from what occurred there among the Indians, it is perhaps that exploitation, unscrupulousness, materialism, and the inhumanity of man to man may pay after all.

NOTES

1. Woodrow Borah and Sherburne F. Cook, *The Aboriginal Population of Central Mexico on the Eve of the Spanish Conquest* (Ibero-Americana, XLV. Berkeley and Los Angeles: University of California Press, 1963).

2. Guardianships over specified numbers of Indians awarded to Spanish conquistadores, who received the tribute and labor of these Indians in return for paying them a living wage and tending to their Christianization and civilization.

3. Forced labor levies. *Mita* was a term applied in Peru, *repartimiento* in Mexico.

4. An Indian community which had been brought together by a member of a religious order. The Jesuit reductions of Paraguay are perhaps the best-known in the Spanish empire.

5. Vincente Murga Sanz, *Juan Ponce de León* (San Juan: Universidad de Puerto Rico, 1959), pp. 100–103.

6. Lewis Hanke, *The Spanish Struggle for Justice in the Conquest of America* (Paperback ed. Boston: Little, Brown, 1965), pp. 31–36.

7. The best general work on the exploration of Florida before 1561 is still Woodbury Lowery, *The Spanish Settlements within the Present Limits of the United States, 1513–1561* (New York and London: G. P. Putnam's Sons, 1911). See also Sanz, *Juan Ponce de León;* Fanny R. Bandelier (tr.), *Journey of Alvar Núñez Cabeza de Vaca* (Chicago: Rio Grande Press, 1964); John Grier Varner and Jeannette J. Varner (trs. and eds.), *The Florida of the Inca,* by Garcilaso de la Vega (Austin: University of Texas, 1951); James A. Robertson (tr. and ed.), *True Relation of the Hardships Suffered by Governor Fernando de Soto & Certain Portuguese Gentlemen During the Discovery of the Province of Florida. Now newly set forth by a Gentleman of Elvas* (2 volumes. Deland: The Florida State Historical Society, 1932–33); Herbert I. Priestley (ed. and tr.), *The Luna Papers: Documents Relating to the Expedition of Don Tristán de Luna y Arellano for the Conquest of La Florida in 1559–1561* (2 volumes. Deland: The Florida State Historical Society, 1928); and Herbert I. Priestley, *Tristán de Luna: Conquistador of the Old South* (Glendale, Calif.: Arthur H. Clark Co., 1936).

8. On Father Cancer and the Dominicans see Victor F. O'Daniel, *Dominicans in Early Florida* (New York: United States Catholic Historical Society, 1930).

9. Lowery, *Spanish Settlements,* p. 376.

10. Quoted in Samuel Eliot Morison, *The European Discovery of America. The Southern Voyages, A.D. 1492–1616* (New York: Oxford University Press, 1974), pp. 66–67.

11. The literature on the Spanish expeditions to Florida in the early part of the sixteenth century is replete with examples of the Indians telling the Spaniards of the golden city or the rich mines to be found farther on in some ill-defined site. This was particularly true of the de Soto expedition. See Varner and Varner (trs. and eds.), *The Florida of the Inca, passim.*

12. On Menéndez see Eugenio Ruidiáz y Caravia, *La Florida: su conquista y colonización por Pedro Menendenez de Aviles* (2 volumes. Madrid, 1893); Genaro García (ed.), *Dos antiguas relaciones de la Florida* (Mexico, 1902); Jeanette Thurber Connor (ed. and tr.), *Pedro Menéndez de Avilés, Adelantado, Governor and Captain-General of Florida. Memorial by Gonzalo Solís de Meras* (Deland: The Florida State Historical Society, 1923).

13. A primary source of documents on the Jesuits is Felix Zubillaga (ed.), *Monumenta antiquae floridae (1566–1572)* (Rome, 1946). See also Felix Zubillaga, *La Florida, la misión jesuitica (1566–1572) y la colonización española* (Rome, 1941), and Michael Kenny, *The Romance of the Floridas* (Milwaukee: Bruce Publishing Co., 1934).

14. Michael V. Gannon, *The Cross in the Sand: The Early Catholic Church in Florida, 1513–1870* (Gainesville: University of Florida Press, 1965), pp. 64–67.

15. John Tate Lanning, *The Spanish Missions of Georgia* (Chapel Hill: University of North Carolina Press, 1935), p. 74.

16. Gannon, *The Cross in the Sand,* pp. 49–67; Lanning, *Spanish Missions,* pp. 168–74.

17. Verner Winslow Crane, *The Southern Frontier, 1670–1732* (Ann Arbor: University of Michigan Press, 1956), pp. 6–36.

18. Gannon, *The Cross in the Sand,* pp. 68–74.

19. John Jay TePaske, *The Governorship of Spanish Florida, 1700–1763* (Durham, N. C.: Duke University Press, 1964), pp. 110–13.

20. *Ibid.*, pp. 113–16, 196–97.

21. Carta del gobernador de la Florida al rey, April 9, 1711, Archivo General de Indias, Audiencia de Santo Domingo, Legajo 843.

22. David H. Corkran, *The Creek Frontier, 1540–1783* (Norman: University of Oklahoma Press, 1967), pp. 57–58.

23. Crane, *Southern Frontier*, pp. 113, 139–40.

24. Corkran, *Creek Frontier*, pp. 75–79; TePaske, *Governorship*, pp. 206–10.

25. TePaske, *Governorship*, pp. 197–209.

26. Corkran, *Creek Frontier*, pp. 83–85, 89–91.

27. *Ibid.*, pp. 85–89.

28. TePaske, *Governorship*, p. 213; Corkran, *Creek Frontier*, pp. 99–102.

29. TePaske, *Governorship*, p. 140.

30. Carta de gobernador de la Florida al rey, March 10, 1740, Archivo General de Indias, Santo Domingo, Legajo 2541; James Oglethorpe to the Duke of Newcastle, Frederica, January 22, 1739/40, London, Public Record Office, C.O. 5:654, pt. 1; TePaske, *Governorship*, pp. 140–44.

31. Corkran, *Creek Frontier*, p. 109.

32. James Oglethorpe to the Duke of Newcastle, Frederica, November 12, 1741, C.O. 5:654, pt. 2; Declaration of the General Heads of the Extraordinaries of the War, January 22, 1742/43, C.O. 5:655, pt. 1.

33. Larry E. Ivers, *British Drums on the Southern Frontier: The Military Colonization of Georgia, 1733–1749* (Chapel Hill: University of North Carolina Press, 1974), pp. 174–76.

34. *Ibid.*, pp. 176–83; Edward Kimber, *A Relation or Journal of a Late Expedition to the Gates of St. Augustine* (London: T. Ashley, 1744).

35. There are no reliable figures on the decline in the Indian population. One writer estimates 14,000 warriors in the area south of the Ohio River and east of the Mississippi in 1763. Of these 14,000, 3,600 were Creeks. This would mean a considerable decline in the population from the seventeenth-century population estimates of the Franciscans. See Jack M. Sosin, *The Revolutionary Frontier, 1763–1783* (New York: Holt, Rinehart, & Winston, 1967), p. 5.

36. For a brief discussion of Spanish policy in the Mississippi Valley for the period 1764–1776, see John Francis Bannon, *The Spanish Borderlands Frontier, 1513–1821* (New York: Holt, Rinehart, & Winston, 1970), pp. 190–95.

37. Corkran, *Creek Frontier*, p. 53.

38. Crane, *Southern Frontier*, p. 113.

39. Gary B. Nash, *Red, White, and Black: The Peoples of Early America* (Englewood Cliffs, N. J.: Prentice-Hall, 1974), p. 107.

40. *Ibid.*, p. 256.

The "Rising French Empire" in the Ohio Valley and Old Northwest
The "Dreaded Juncture of the French Settlements in Canada with those of Louisiana"

GEORGE A. RAWLYK

In July, 1608, Samuel de Champlain established a French settlement at Quebec. From this tiny bridgehead, the French North American empire would slowly spread westward into the Great Lakes area, the Mississippi and western Canadian prairie. Unable to find the precious metals for which they desperately were searching in the early seventeenth century, most of the French colonists were content to involve themselves in the fur trade and in subsistence agriculture. The Roman Catholic Church, however, saw in the French colonial venture a heavensent opportunity to convert thousands of North American Indians to the Christian faith.*

Despite the ravages of the Iroquois and the heavy losses from disease, the population of New France grew from a handful of original colonists in 1608 to some 2,500 in 1663, 6,500 in 1668, 16,000 in 1700, 25,000 in 1721, and almost 60,000 in the 1750s.[1] This population expansion was largely the result of an unusually high birthrate, not an aggressive French colonizing policy. In fact, the French authorities did very little to encourage emigration to New France after 1670.

It had been the intention of Louis XIV and his colonial officials to fashion on the banks of the St. Lawrence River a society which the king could completely control. It was to be a colony where order and stability would be ensured by carefully and precisely defining the roles each person was to play within the colonial society. Three major institutions—the colonial government, the seigneurial system, and the Roman Catholic Church—were to be the means by which stability and social discipline would be imposed upon the colony. These institutions,

George A. Rawlyk, a specialist in the history of the Atlantic Maritime Provinces, is Professor of History, Queens University, Kingston, Ontario, Canada.

*The author is very much indebted to Mr. Olaf Janzen for his considerable help in preparing this paper.

however, were not successful in achieving this goal. By the middle of the eighteenth century, instead of the desired docility there was what has been referred to as a "spirit of independence"[2] in New France; instead of being firmly tied to a simple agrarian existence, many French Canadians had found freedom and excitement on the frontier by acting as middlemen in the fur trade. Others had flocked to the rapidly expanding towns in the colony—to Quebec, Montreal, and Trois Rivières—where officials complained there was widespread "frivolity" and an "aversion to assiduous and regular labour."[3]

Together with the influence of the North American environment and the French heritage, the governmental framework, the seigneurial system, and the church—despite their collective failure to create the ideal colony—significantly shaped the contours of French-Canadian development and molded its unique characteristics. The governmental framework imposed upon New France was not a formidable instrument of oppression. It is quite wrong to assert, as did the influential historian Francis Parkman, that "an ignorant population, sprung from a brave and active race, but trained to subjection and dependence through centuries of feudal and monarchical despotism was planted in the wilderness by the hand of authority."[4] Rather, in New France, government assumed a character more paternalistic than despotic. Over and over again the governors of New France were instructed by the monarch to treat the colonists with "gentleness and goodness" and with "an enlightened mildness."[5]

The question immediately comes to mind—why had the metropolitan authority become so paternalistic in New France? There appear to be two main reasons which also help to explain why the seigneurial system was significantly modified on being transplanted to the New World. First, since during almost all of the pre-Conquest period the colony was obsessed with increasing its population, the governmental authorities felt compelled to temper their absolutism in order to encourage immigration and to discourage existing settlers from abandoning their farms for the fur frontier. And second, almost from the beginnings of settlement, the colonists shrewdly realized the strength of their bargaining position. Consequently, they were able to squeeze a relatively great deal of freedom from officials who were afraid of losing their support and goodwill.

By the middle of the eighteenth century the inhabitants of New France, whether living in town or country, had developed certain traits that clearly distinguished them from their brethren in France. Such a broad gulf had come into being that Colonel Louis-Antoine de Bougainville, Lieutenant-General Louis-Joseph Montcalm's aide, commented in 1756: "It seems that we [the French] are of a different nation,

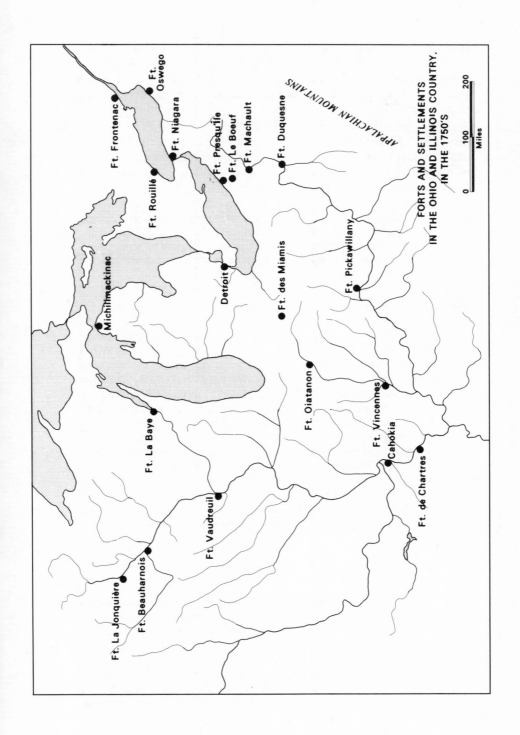

FORTS AND SETTLEMENTS IN THE OHIO AND ILLINOIS COUNTRY, IN THE 1750'S

even an enemy one."[6] Seven years earlier during a visit to France a Madame Bégon arrived at the same general conclusion: "It seems here I don't know how people ought to live and that I am nothing but an Iroquois." She went on, "if I can once get home, I shall be happy indeed."[7]

What were the main characteristics of the so-called French-Canadian mentality? Perhaps this question can be best answered by referring to the observations made by four men at different times regarding the character of the inhabitants of New France. In 1685 the Baron de Lahontan described the inhabitants thus:

> [They] are a robust, brawny, well-made people, they are strong, vigorous, active, brave, and indefatigable; in a word, they want nothing but the knowledge of polite Letters. They are presumptuous, and very full of themselves; they value themselves beyond all the nations of the Earth.[8]

The noted Jesuit Father Charlevoix in 1720 observed that:

> The Canadians, that is to say, the Creoles of Canada, breathe at their Birth an Air of Liberty, which makes them very agreeable in the Commerce of Life, and our Language is no where spoken with greater Purity.... There is nobody rich here, and 'tis Pity, for they love to live generously, and no one thinks of laying up Riches. ... They are of good stature, and have the best complexions in the world in both sexes. A pleasant humour, and agreeable and polite manners are common to all. ...
> How many gentlemen in all the provinces in France would envy the common inhabitants in Canada if they knew it. ... I know not whether I should place among the failings of the Canadian, the good opinion they have of themselves. ... We must allow, on the other hand, that they have excellent qualities. They are of good stature, and well shaped in body. ... Their agility and dexterity are without parallel.[9]

Then in the 1730s Intendant Gilles Hocquart remarked:

> The Canadians are fond of distinctions and attentions, plume themselves on their courage, and are extremely sensitive to slights or the smallest corrections. They are self-interested, vindictive, prone to drunkenness, use a great deal of brandy, and pass for not being at all truthful. This portrait is true of many of them, particularly the country people: those of the towns are less vicious. They are all attached to religion, and criminals are rare. They are volatile . . . which prevents their succeeding as they might in farming and trade.

They have not the rude and rustic air of our French peasants. If they are put on their honour and governed with justice, they are tractable enough; but their natural disposition is indocile.[10]

Finally, in 1749 Peter Kalm, the famous Swedish traveler, wrote:

The common man in Canada is more civilized and clever than in any other place of the world that I have visited. On entering one of the peasants' houses, no matter where, and on beginning to talk with the men and women, one is quite amazed at the good breeding and courteous answers which are received, no matter what the question is. . . . Frenchmen who were born in Paris said themselves that one never finds in France among country people the courtesy and good breeding which one observes here.[11]

By the middle of the eighteenth century, a French-Canadian type, physically strong, independent, devout, friendly, gay, somewhat vain and sometimes lazy had evidently come into being.[12] This type, it should be stressed, had been molded by the interaction of three significant forces—the immigrant mind, the North American physical environment, and the political, religious and economic institutions of New France. A decade before the Conquest, the inhabitants of the Valley of the St. Lawrence had become "French Canadians"; they had appropriated what has been called "a moral being, a collective identity" and had evolved into "a new nation."[13]

Despite the American propaganda barrage concerning the "Rising French Empire" and despite the widespread fear of "French Encirclement,"[14] few inhabitants of pre-Conquest New France manifested any real interest in westward imperial expansion. There was more than enough empty space for them to fill in the St. Lawrence Valley. It is not surprising, therefore, that until nearly the middle of the eighteenth century the Ohio Valley was almost totally ignored by the French authorities. It is true, of course, that after 1701 the French had theoretically adopted a new policy of territorial expansion designed to exclude the Anglo-Americans from the interior of North America. This policy was implemented by creating Louisiana and by constructing fortifications in the Illinois country. The Ohio Valley, however, was almost completely bypassed. In fact, the upper reaches of the Ohio were not even explored by the French until Léry's expedition did so in 1729. At this same time, it should be pointed out, La Vérendrye was already planning his explorations in search of the "western sea."[15]

In 1721 the British Board of Trade finally responded to news about French expansion south of the Great Lakes by urging the building of fortifications on the Great Lakes and in the Allegheny passes. But little of consequence was actually done by the British to block the French. In 1726 Fort Oswego was built on Lake Ontario but nothing was done about the Allegheny passes, and the Ohio Valley was as much ignored by the British as it was by the French.[16]

In view of this record of inactivity in the Ohio Valley, it seems both remarkable and ironic that, in the short space of ten years from 1744 to 1754, French interest and behavior in the Ohio country, together with the growing Anglo-American fear of French encirclement, would play such a key role in precipitating hostilities between France and England. The apparent change in French policy seemed to many contemporaries to have been very dramatic. Yet a closer examination of developments in the Ohio country during this period reveals not so much a sudden change in policy as a logical extension of the policy which for decades had guided French activities in North America.

This policy recognized that the fur trade remained the economic pillar of New France. Centered at Montreal, this trade accounted for two thirds of all French-Canadian exports during the first half of the eighteenth century even though agriculture and industry were receiving considerable governmental assistance. The French policy also, it should be pointed out, recognized the relative paucity of settlers in the French North American colonies. Consequently, it was realized that the success of French colonial enterprises in North America was based on a careful cultivation of the various Indian nations. By this means the French had succeeded in obtaining both furs and much-needed allies. It is interesting to note that the French governmental authorities actively participated in implementing this policy. Forts Frontenac, Niagara, and Detroit were maintained as King's posts; goods were sold below cost there in order to entice the Indians away from English posts such as Fort Oswego. Every year a portion of the profits earned from the sale of *congés* and post leases was spent on presents for the Indians to keep them loyal and passive. And before the outbreak of the War of the Austrian Succession in 1744, this policy had, it seems clear, helped guarantee the neutrality or pro-French stance of most of the Indians inhabiting the region south of the Great Lakes.[17]

Nevertheless, such a policy had some obvious weaknesses; one of these was the dangerous French dependence on an uninterrupted flow of trade goods with which to purchase the continued friendship of the Indians. During the War of the Austrian Succession, from 1744 to 1748, this flow was seriously blocked by British naval supremacy in the North Atlantic. As early as 1745, French colonial officials predicted that their Indian allies would automatically turn to Anglo-American traders once the French were not able to satisfy their needs. The commandant of Detroit pointed out in July, 1745, that the English at Fort Oswego were spreading rumors to the Indians traveling to Montreal that the French would soon be short of trade supplies.[18] Within two years the English had made good this threat, and the French post commanders found themselves confronted by a serious dilemma. Their efforts to buy the active assistance of the Indians in the Illinois country for attacks on the Anglo-Americans, who had penetrated the region in force after 1743, had collapsed because they had nothing with which to make payments to their allies. In disgust and out of need, the Indians began to turn to the very people the French detested and feared—the Anglo-Americans.[19]

Despite these real threats to French policy, some of the French colonial officials, at least in their letters, showed confidence and optimism. Obviously they were eager to impress the minister of Marine that they were still in control of events.[20] However, by the summer of 1747 they could no longer avoid the harsh realities of the new situation. It had become clear to the distraught French post commanders at Detroit and in the Illinois country that a general Indian uprising against the French was being planned. The Anglo-American traders at Sandusky and the area of the Greater Miami River had been extremely active in 1746 and 1747 in drawing many of the Indians away from the French. They had fully exploited the scarcity of French goods and also the Anglo-American victory at Louisbourg in 1745. If the so-called "French Gibraltar of North America" could be captured by a motley collection of Yankees and if the British fleet could virtually drive the French navy from the North Atlantic, the Indians could expect little assistance from their traditional allies. Not only did the Anglo-American traders drive home this point about the shattered French prestige and power, but they also cleverly played on fears of the Ottawa, Potawatomi, Hurons, Chippewa, and Miami, concerning imminent raids by the Iroquois, who were known to be sympathetic to the English. In addition, the Anglo-Americans gave presents to the Indians in an attempt to win them over. These policies were so successful that by the middle of 1747 the Hurons near Detroit were preparing a surprise attack on that settlement. Other tribes, it was hoped, would join in and sweep the upper country and the Illinois country free of the French. Only a fortuitous discovery of the plan by the Baron de Longueuil, the commandant of Detroit, enabled the French to prepare for the uprising and to summon help.[21]

The so-called "Conspiracy of 1747" was nipped in the bud largely because of the arrival of a shipment of trade goods at Detroit, together with an impressive military escort. Once the Indian attack plan was aborted, most of the Indians made loud declarations of loyalty to the French. And soon the correspondence of the colonial administrators regained its earlier sense of optimism.[22]

Nevertheless, this incident had a significant impact on the French and on their policy. As might be expected, the French officials recognized that one of the principal causes of the unrest had been the Anglo-American activities among the Indians.[23] And, furthermore, the refusal of the traditional French-Indian allies to help suppress the uprising persuaded at least the Marquis de La Galissonière, the governor of Canada from 1747 to 1749, that never again should the French allow themselves to be caught in a position where they were forced to rely on the co-operation of Indians: "I think that one of the best ways of forestalling in the future any similar disorder would be to settle a good number of husbandmen at Detroit. Thus that post would be in a condition to subsist almost entirely of itself and to defend all the posts which are nearby." At this point, La Galissonière introduced for the first time the contention that the real threat to the Illinois country came from uncontested Anglo-American access to the Ohio Valley: "I think that is the only way of preventing the English from establishing themselves on the Ohio River, an establishment quite capable of interrupting our communication with the Mississippi which is almost necessary to both colonies."[24]

Here, then, is a statement of the fundamental impact which the "Conspiracy of 1747" had on French policy in North America. Most of the Indians had indicated in no uncertain terms that their support would go to whichever power exhibited the greater military and commercial strength and prestige. Prestige in this sense rested on the ability to maintain a firm grip on trade in the interior, an ability which the French could no longer be certain of exercising in the face of growing British seapower. Unable, therefore, to rely in future on being able to outbid the English for the co-operation and support of the Indians, the French were compelled to consider the alternative—barring the Anglo-Americans from the interior of the continent altogether. The Comte de Raymond, commanding officer at Fort des Miamis, suggested that this be done through diplomatic channels. More realistically, La Galissonière focused his attention on what could actually be done to plug the Anglo-American conduit to the interior—the Ohio Valley. The geophysical characteristics of the region, it was argued, were such that the existing troops of New France were capable of blocking the Ohio Valley without depending on the Indians for support.[25]

La Galissonière's recommendations impressed his superior, the Comte de Maurepas. For some time, the minister of Marine had been reconsidering the decision of 1717 which had placed the Illinois country under the jurisdiction of Louisiana. The agricultural benefits to be had from the Illinois country during the 1730s and 1740s did not seem worth the cost of spreading out even thinner the meager military resources of Louisiana. La Galissonière, in October 1747, had suggested that, in terms of North American strategic realities, the Illinois country and New France were crucially linked by means of the Ohio Valley. French control of the Ohio was seen to be the key to continued French control of the Illinois country. And it seemed obvious to La Galissonière that only New France could effectively control the Ohio Valley.

Even though he was impressed with La Galissonière's analysis, Maurepas demanded more information about the French presence in the Illinois country. Both La Galissonière and the Marquis de Vaudreuil, governor of Louisiana, responded to the demand, but La Galissonière's study of the problem probably proved to be the more influential of the two. The governor of New France acknowledged in 1748 that the Illinois country was indeed an economic drain on France, offering no prospect of immediate financial return. This disarming candour was more effective than Vaudreuil's protestations concerning the economic necessity of preserving the Illinois-Louisiana connection. La Galissonière's understanding of the importance of the Illinois country was, in contrast, based on an evaluation of the region in terms of its strategic importance in preserving the French Empire in North America. The territory was, he argued, an important link connecting Louisiana and New France. It stood as a barrier to Anglo-American expansion which might otherwise threaten even Mexico. A strong French presence in the Illinois country, he contended, would impress the Indians, win their allegiance, and permit the use of the region as a base for attack against the Anglo-American colonies. La Galissonière concluded that these recommendations required not simply stronger French-Indian ties but rather substantially more French settlers and troops. (By 1752 the French population in the Illinois country was approximately only fifteen hundred.)[26] La Galissonière envisaged a major colonizing effort which would establish a commanding French presence in the region— a presence which would undoubtedly make further reliance on the Indians unnecessary.[27]

La Galissonière's proposals earned what some would consider to be undeserved praise, both from his contemporaries and from most historians. In a way, of course, his proposals were strategically shrewd. Yet they were neither as realistic nor as original as La Galissonière's admirers would like to believe. The proposals were unrealistic because France had never before succeeded in mounting a sustained immigration and settlement program in North America. They were also unrealistic because the Indians would never have tolerated a major settlement program. One of the few advantages which the French had over the English in North America was that their frontier posts were never transformed into major settlements. Some of them, to be sure, supported small-scale European communities; but these were always designed merely to add to the military strength and security of the post. The Indians had made clear their attitude towards settlement; the English understood this and so did most of the French. Thus, La Galissonière's grandiose proposals were at odds with reality.[28]

Nor were his proposals particularly original. La Galissonière's predecessor, the Marquis de Beauharnois and Intendant Gilles Hocquart had both endorsed the suggestion that the agricultural settlement at Detroit be expanded. La Galissonière had consulted with Beauharnois after arriving at Quebec on September 19, 1747, and before the departure of Beauharnois for France on October 14, 1747. This gave La Galissonière more than enough time to seize upon the idea of an expanded program of settlement and apply it to a major western policy recommendation. There is also more than a strong likelihood that La Galissonière's interpretation of the strategical value of the Illinois country was in part inspired by Maurepas' letter of February 23, 1748. The minister of Marine, in that letter, had expressed fear that the anti-French community of Indians under La Demoiselle in the Illinois country "might easily interrupt communication between Canada and Louisiana, and even occasion the loss of the greater part of the posts of both Colonies."[29]

Thus, not only were La Galissonière's recommendations unsound, but they may also have been carefully tailored to please the minister of Marine. However, by the time La Galissonière's famous letter of September 1, 1748, reached Versailles, Maurepas had been replaced by Antoine-Louis Rouillé, Comte de Jouy.[30] Unfamiliar with the mechanics and priorities of his new office, Rouillé decided to delay indefinitely any decision of returning Illinois to Canadian jurisdiction.[31] Yet it should be pointed out that his every action indicated that Rouillé had adopted Maurepas' decision to rely less in future on Indian allies and more on developing and exploiting New France's own resources. It is not surprising, therefore, that in a letter to the newly appointed governor of Canada, the Marquis de la Jonquière, before the latter's departure for North America in the spring of 1749, Rouillé expressed his pleasure that the Indian "Conspiracy of 1747" had been suppressed by a show of force: "As a rule, you will find the officers disposed to put an end to quarrels with the savages by means of conciliation; but it is certain, and experience has at all times proved it, that they can be restrained only by well-advised examples of severity, and you must not neglect any opportunity of making them."[32] The new minister of Marine also proposed implementing a new settlement program along the lines suggested earlier by Beauharnois, Hocquart, and La Galissonière to strengthen the interior.[33]

Between the time of sending his letter to Maurepas in September, 1748, and his return to France a year later, La Galissonière began to put his words into action. His recommendations to Maurepas had dealt exclusively with the Illinois country; the Ohio Valley had not even been discussed. However, La Galissonière had not deliberately ignored that key area; rather, he naïvely believed that a modest French military show of force would be enough to win back the support of the Indians, to frighten away the Anglo-American interlopers, and to assert, once and for all, France's claim to the Ohio Valley. Consequently, in order to implement this policy, in the middle of June, 1749, a force of 180 Canadians and 35 troops and officers, under the command of Pierre-Joseph Céloron de Blainville, made its way to the Ohio Valley. The expedition was to accomplish its goals by assembling Indians at strategic places to witness the ceremonial burying of lead plates recording the historic event. Céloron was ordered by La Galissonière "to drive out the Hurons" who had participated in the "Conspiracy of 1747," and also "to win back some other Indians who have departed from their duty, as well as to remove the English who come to trade in those regions."[34]

La Galissonière entertained great hopes for the Céloron expedition, but these hopes were never realized. In retrospect it seems strange that the often perceptive governor failed to realize that such a force was just too small to intimidate the Indians or to frighten the Anglo-American traders. Moreover, he should have realized that the expedition was just a little too large to be construed by the Indians as anything but a threat and an insult to them. La Galissonière can be criticized for these and other things, but he cannot really be criticized for his misreading of the Anglo-American threat. In September, 1748, the Ohio Company had been formed, and this development significantly strengthened the determination of the Anglo-American traders (who in many instances doubled as agents for the land company) to maintain their hold on the valley and its natives. Consequently, La Jonquière, who had replaced La Galissonière before Céloron returned, sadly concluded that "the mission of the Sieur de Céloron to la Belle Rivière [the Ohio River] had had quite a different effect from that expected by Monsieur the Comte de la Galissonière; that, on the contrary, the nations have gathered together in that region, that they are in greater numbers and more angry than ever against the French; and that, although he summoned the English to withdraw and forbade them to come back, they nevertheless continue their trade with those nations and even urge them to attack the French."[35]

La Jonquière had soon come to realize that the French hold on the Ohio-Illinois country was still tenuous and that a continuation of the policy adopted and implemented by La Galissonière could only weaken substantially the French position there. Throughout the Ohio Valley and the Illinois country and beyond, the Indians were very restless and were giving every indication of conspiring once again to try to drive the French from that territory. The new center of the anti-French movement was La Demoiselle's Miami village on the Great Miami River. By 1750 the Anglo-Americans had established a trading post there called Pickawillany, and they had quickly become the predominant influence in the new Indian intrigue. Early in 1750 reports began to circulate among various French post commanders and officials about the possible imminent Miami and Shawnee attacks.[36]

Rouillé, when informed of these rumors, urged La Jonquière to put an end to the unrest by persuading the Shawnee allies of La Demoiselle to leave the Ohio Valley.[37] But La Jonquière was also instructed that he must not under any circumstances become involved in any disputes with the Indians.[38] "The question," wrote Rouillé some time later

> is not to operate against the Indians, but to prevent the interloping trade the English are driving in a country belonging to us, and which, previous to the last war, they would be careful not to dispute with us; this is proposed to be effected by checking at the same time the views they entertain of establishing posts there. It is easy, therefore, to render the Indians indifferent in this regard; nay, even to induce them to understand that for the sake of their own tranquility and of the freedom of their trade, in which we have never clogged them, they must wish that we should stop the progress of the English scheme.[39]

It may have seemed an "easy" task for Rouillé from his safe French vantage point; but for La Jonquière the situation was an extremely difficult one. On the one hand, he was expected to pacify hostile Indians without using force, and on the other hand he was expected to turn these same Indians against their intimate trading partners, the Anglo-Americans, also without using force. What the minister of Marine failed to realize was that the respect of the Indians could only be assured by convincing them that French power was superior to British power. And, as many French Canadians could tell him, such a policy called for a strong show of force and plenty of supplies.[40]

Given the circumstances and his instructions, Governor La Jonquière did his best to strengthen the French position in North America. Fort Rouillé (Toronto) was established in 1750 in order to intercept the Indian trade flowing to Fort Oswego. The post at Michilimackinac was strengthened and forts were built at Sault Ste. Marie and at the foot of the Niagara portage. Diplomatic negotiations in 1750 and 1751 secured the neutrality of the Cayuga and Onondaga; these tribes had, following La Galissonière's activities in 1749, feared that the French were eager to force the withdrawal of all Indians from the Ohio Valley. La Jonquière reassured them, promising that "The French, who will go to the Beautiful river, will carry wherewith to supply the wants of those who are there, and will be careful not to disturb them." Only those who proved hostile to the French, declared the governor, would be in danger of expulsion.[41] Finally, in an effort to determine more precisely what was happening in the Ohio country, the governor sent Captain Philippe de Joncaire with a small party to that region.[42]

Despite these efforts, which remained within the limits set by La Jonquière's instructions, the reports sent back by Joncaire and other French officers in the interior indicated that a passive policy would not work. During 1751, at least nine Frenchmen and two slaves were killed in isolated incidents south of Lake Erie. Rumors were circulating of conferences attended by Illinois, Miami, Delawares, Shawnee, Iroquois, and Anglo-American traders. Tension increased when a bad harvest created a scarcity of provisions. Joncaire sadly reported that "the Indians of the Beautiful river are all English."[43]

Faced with this rapidly deteriorating situation, La Jonquière was receptive to any plans offering firm measures against the hostile Indians of the Ohio Valley, especially those at Pickawillany. One proposal came in 1751 from the Abbé Picquet who was in charge of the Mission of La Présentation (near present-day Ogdensburg, New York). Picquet was on good terms with all of the Iroquois except the Mohawks, and proposed pushing into the Ohio Valley in the following year with seven hundred Iroquois and five hundred domiciled Indians. Once in the Ohio country, they would be reinforced by two thousand Choctaws and six hundred more Iroquois. This huge Indian army would then clear the Ohio country of the Anglo-Americans while suppressing the Miami revolt at the same time. This plan, of course, was totally opposed to the policy set down in La Jonquière's instructions which prohibited using Indians to enforce French rule and fomenting an Indian war. Nevertheless, the governor, together with François Bigot, the intendant, and Longueuil, the governor of Montreal, approved of the plan.[44]

It is not clear to what extent La Jonquière was influenced by French Canadians such as Bigot and Longueuil. There is evidence that aggressive measures were preferred by these men. In addition, it was well known that the French-Canadian *habitants*, who were firmly attached to their land along the St. Lawrence, were opposed to being involved in any way in military campaigns in the Ohio Valley.[45] And, consequently, an expedition such as that proposed by Abbé Picquet would strike a very responsive chord with them, since the Indians, not the *habitants*, could do the dirty work for the agents of French imperialism.

The expedition was not, however, to the liking of Rouillé, who had the plan canceled. This development did not discourage La Jonquière, who then proceeded to draw up a proposal for a combined Indian-French campaign against the Miami. Separate detachments of French troops and Indian allies were to be sent to the southwest, to rendezvous in the spring and descend suddenly on La Demoiselle's Indian "republic." But once again the plan had to be abandoned. This time the Indians at Detroit were to blame, for they were unconvinced that the plan would work and so they would not co-operate. La Jonquière held Céloron de Blainville, who was now commandant of Detroit, partly responsible for having misled him about the willingness and enthusiasm of the Indians to participate.[46]

La Jonquière never had another opportunity to suppress the Indians of the Ohio country. Following an unrelated dispute with Rouillé, he resigned his offices, and before he could return to France, he died, in March, 1752. His replacement, the Marquis Duquesne, was still in France, and so the administration of the colony fell temporarily into the hands of Longueuil, the governor of Montreal.[47]

During his brief term in office, Longueuil attempted to continue La Jonquière's efforts to suppress the Indian unrest in the interior. He proposed sending a force of four hundred French troops to Detroit that summer, to be followed in the spring of the following year by a slightly larger force. Sometime in 1753, according to the plan, the approximately eight-hundred-man force would then overpower and overawe the hostile Miami and drive out the Anglo-Americans. This plan, in its strategic thrust, was quite similar to La Jonquière's plan of 1751. It differed, of course, in one fundamental way! Longueuil explicitly excluded the Indians from participating. The unco-operative behavior of the Indians domiciled at Detroit in 1751 may have persuaded him not to use any Indians. Or it may have been that Longueuil, expecting the Indians to join the French expedition once they saw its size, deliberately excluded any mention of them because he did not want to alienate his superior.[48]

While Longueuil labored hard to try to put his plan into effect in the summer of 1752, a force of 250 Chippewa Indians from Michilimackinac, under the command of Charles-Michel Mouet de Langlade, had taken the initiative and had attacked and destroyed Pickawillany. La Demoiselle, the Miami chief who had caused so much trouble for the French, was permanently removed from the scene by the simple expedient of boiling and eating him. The terror of a smallpox epidemic contributed further to the collapse of the Indian unrest in the Ohio and Illinois country.[49]

Even before the news of the Langlade expedition had reached him, Rouillé was expressing his displeasure with the extent to which La Jonquière and Longueuil had ignored his orders to avoid entanglements with the Indians. The minister of Marine was determined that the new governor of New France should clearly understand his wishes and conscientiously carry them out. Duquesne was, therefore, warned to ignore the advice of these French Canadians who wanted him to continue the policy of La Jonquière and Longueuil.[50]

Consequently, when Duquesne arrived in New France, he was committed to implementing a military policy independent of Indian allies. He immediately made plans to occupy the upper Ohio Valley in force in order to bar English access to the country and the Indians beyond. An expedition was organized, and in 1753, over two thousand Frenchmen (300 Troupes de la Marine and 1,700 Canadian militia) advanced into the area south of Lake Erie and into the upper reaches of the Ohio Valley. Forts were erected and garrisoned, roads were built, and when the Anglo-Americans tried to protest or resist, they were packed on their way.[51]

This was more than the English colonial governments had bargained for, but most were not keen to finance countermeasures. Nevertheless, a small military force under the command of George Washington, financed by the Virginia House of Burgesses, set out early in 1754 in an effort to force the French to withdraw. The result was rather an ignoble defeat for Washington—but a defeat with major consequences. The mother countries began to participate directly in these affairs, with the result that the Seven Years' War between France and England began, to all intents and purposes, not in 1756 but rather in 1754 in the forested mountain country of the upper Ohio Valley.

What, then, can be said about French policy in the Ohio-Illinois country? La Jonquière, influenced by Canadians such as Longueuil and Bigot, had tried to preserve French authority in the region by forcing the Indians to co-operate. This policy depended on the active assistance of allied Indians. It was a policy rooted in the belief that an exercise of French power and prestige would draw the Indians away from the Anglo-American traders who had already penetrated the territory. But the French ministry of Marine was adamantly opposed to this policy. Maurepas and Rouillé both believed that the expulsion of the Anglo-American traders was the major objective. This could be achieved, they thought, by mounting exclusively French military operations against the traders; no Indian allies would be necessary. As far as they were concerned, the "Conspiracy of 1747" had underscored the fact that the Indians were not to be trusted.

Superficially, the latter policy seemed to be the more effective of the two. Duquesne's expedition, mounted without the help of Indians, had evidently impressed the native inhabitants of the Ohio Valley. Moreover, it had succeeded in sealing the English out of the Ohio country. Thus, it may be argued that the success of the expedition seemed to justify Rouillé's arguments.

Yet Duquesne's accomplishments were not won in isolation nor were they achieved without great cost. The 1752 attack on Pickawillany and the smallpox epidemic had made Duquesne's task that much easier. Yet it must not be forgotten that Duquesne lost four hundred men to disease just in building his road to the Ohio from Lake Erie. This huge cost in human lives confirmed the worst fears of the French Canadians who had opposed the expedition.[52] But most important of all, Duquesne's efforts, by not only claiming but also occupying the upper Ohio Valley, directly threatened the English colonies in North America and helped spark the "Great War for the Empire." La Jonquière's attempts to secure the Illinois country by pacifying the restless Indians through intrigue, diplomacy, and the help of allied Indians probably would not have provoked Great Britain into war. The French Canadians, as has been pointed out earlier, had little interest in the Ohio Valley, except for the few who resented the Anglo-Americans' use of it as a base from which they threatened the Illinois and upper country.

Thus, the metropolitan French perception of the Ohio Valley and the Illinois country had, by 1749, led to the adoption of a policy directed towards the military occupation of the region. Although this was a policy which ran counter to the wishes of many influential French Canadians, it was, nevertheless, only a variant of the policy which had guided French activities in North America for decades. That policy had enabled the French to expand into and exploit the interior of North America without occupying it with settlements. Instead, the French had relied on the respect and co-operation of the Indians. The imperial objectives of France and the commercial objectives of New France were compatibly expressed within the framework of this policy. However, when the commercial disruption caused by the War of the Austrian Succession undermined the co-operation of the Indians, it also undermined the faith of French administrators in the wisdom of that policy. And, consequently, the policy was modified. Reliance on the Indians was discouraged, settlement of the interior was favored, and military operations against the Anglo-Americans were promoted.

Some French Canadians, at least, realized the basic dangers involved in such a policy. It represented, among other things, the abandonment of the traditional French-Canadian approach to North American realities. Metropolitan France was imposing its special brand of ignorance on the affairs of New France. The Conquest owed more to this policy than it did to historical inevitability. As Professor William J. Eccles has observed, "Ineptitude in the French military command and government at home, and the fortunes of war, gave Britain dominion over the vast

French territory."[53] It was, it should be pointed out, a close thing. Had Montcalm not adopted such foolish tactics at Quebec on September 13, 1759, the British army might have been destroyed and New France, including the Illinois country, at least, might have remained French territory. But for how long? Historians, of course, must deal with what happened and not with what might have happened. By 1760 the "Dreaded Juncture of the French Settlements in Canada with those of Louisiana"[54] had been dealt a fatal blow. The French-Canadian nation would have to be satisfied with the somewhat restrictive provincial boundaries of Quebec rather than those of a transcontinental Gallic country.

NOTES

1. Georges Langlois, *Histoire de la Population Canadienne-Française* (Montreal: A. Levesque, 1934), p. 75.

2. Guy Frégault, *La Civilisation de la Nouvelle-France (1713–1744)* (Montreal: Société des éditions Pascal, 1944), p. 175.

3. Quoted in Mason Wade, *The French Canadians, 1760–1945* (Toronto: Macmillan, 1956), p. 41.

4. Francis Parkman, *The Old Regime in Canada* (Boston: Little, Brown, and Co., 1901), p. 461. For a radically different view see A. L. Burt, "The Frontier in the History of New France," in Canadian Historical Association *Report* (1940), pp. 93–99.

5. Quoted in Frégault, *La Civilisation de la Nouvelle-France*, p. 135.

6. Quoted in Wade, *The French Canadians*, p. 43.

7. Quoted in Arthur R. M. Lower, *Canadians in the Making* (Toronto: Longmans, Green, 1958), p. 78.

8. Reuben G. Thwaites (ed.), *Lahontan's New Voyages to North America* (2 volumes. Chicago: A. C. McClurg & Co., 1905), I, 391.

9. Pierre F. Charlevoix, *A Voyage to North-America* (2 volumes. Dublin: J. Exshaw, and J. Potts, 1766), I, 37, 139-40.

10. Quoted in Parkman, *The Old Regime in Canada*, pp. 455–56.

11. Adolph B. Benson (ed.), *Peter Kalm's Travels in North America* (2 volumes. New York: Wilson-Erickson, Inc., 1937), II, 558.

12. Gérard Filteau, *La Naissance d'Une Nation* (2 volumes. Montreal, 1937), II, 217-30.

13. Guy Frégault, *Canadian Society in the French Regime* (Ottawa: Canadian Historical Association, 1956), p. 15.

14. E. F. O'Neill, "English Fear of French Encirclement in North America, 1680–1763" (Ph.D. dissertation, University of Michigan, 1941). See also Richard W. Van Alstyne, *The Rising American Empire* (New York: Oxford University Press, 1960), pp. 10–27.

15. Max Savelle, *The Diplomatic History of the Canadian Boundary, 1749–1763* (New Haven: Yale University Press, 1940), pp. 9–10.

16. Van Alstyne, *The Rising American Empire*, pp. 13–14.

17. William J. Eccles, *France in America* (Toronto: Fitzhenry and Whiteside, 1973), pp. 119-20.

18. See for example Longueuil, commandant of Detroit, to Governor Beau-

harnois, July 28, 1745, *Wisconsin Historical Collections*, XVII (1906), 446–47. Excellent biographical information as well as background material for this essay is to be found in the recently published *Dictionary of Canadian Biography*, III: *1741 to 1770* (Toronto, 1974).

19. Harold A. Innis, *The Fur Trade in Canada* (Toronto: University of Toronto Press, 1956), p. 116; Albert T. Volwiler, *George Croghan and the Westward Movement, 1741–1782* (Cleveland: The Arthur H. Clark Co., 1926), p. 42; Beauharnois to Maurepas, October 28, 1745, *Wisconsin Historical Collections*, XII (1892), 449; Vaudreuil to Maurepas, March 22 and April 8, 1747, *Illinois Historical Collections*, XXIX (1940), 15, 21–22. For further information on the Anglo-American penetration into the Illinois country see Savelle, *The Diplomatic History of the Canadian Boundary, 1749–1763*, p. 12.

20. See for example Vaudreuil to Maurepas, March 22 and April 8, 1747, in *Illinois Historical Collections*, XXIX, 14, 22.

21. Gustave Lanctot, *A History of Canada* (Volume 1 – . Toronto: Clarke, Irwin, 1963–), III, 73; George F. G. Stanley, *New France: The Last Phase 1744–1760* (Toronto: McClelland and Stewart, 1968), pp. 29–30; William J. Eccles, *The Canadian Frontier 1534–1760* (New York: Holt, Rinehart, & Winston, 1969), p. 154. See also the Report of M. Boishebert on Indian Affairs, November, 1747, in Edmund B. O'Callaghan (ed.), *Documents Relative to the Colonial History of the State of New York* (15 volumes. Albany, 1856–87), X, 83 (hereafter cited as *New York Colonial Documents*); Journal of Occurrences in Canada, 1746–1747, *ibid.*, X, 89–132; Journal of Occurrences in Canada, 1747–1748, *ibid.*, X, 137–45; Vaudreuil to Maurepas, April 8 and September 19, 1747, *Illinois Historical Collections*, XXIX, 22, 31–35; de Raymond to Maurepas, November 2, 1747, *Wisconsin Historical Collections*, XVII (1906), 474–75.

22. La Galissonière to Maurepas, October 22, 1747, *Illinois Historical Collections*, XXIX, 38–39; Abstract of La Galissonière's Despatches, April 8, 1748, *New York Colonial Documents*, X, 133.

23. Vaudreuil to Maurepas, March 22, 1747, *Illinois Historical Collections*, XXIX, 16–17; La Galissonière to Maurepas, October 22, 1747, *ibid.*, pp. 38–39; de Raymond to Maurepas, November 2, 1747, *ibid.*, pp. 43–46.

24. La Galissonière to Maurepas, October 22, 1747, *Illinois Historical Collections*, XXIX, 38–39.

25. De Raymond to Maurepas, November 2, 1747, *Wisconsin Historical Collections*, XVII, 476.

26. Guy Frégault, *Le Grand Marquis: Pierre de Rigaud de Vaudreuil et la Louisiane* (Montreal: Fides, 1952), pp. 129–30.

27. Maurepas to Vaudreuil, April 25, 1748, *Illinois Historical Collections*, XXIX, 61–66; Maurepas to La Galissonière, April 25, 1748, *Wisconsin Historical Collections*, XVIII (1908), 14–17; La Galissonière to Maurepas, September 1, 1748, *ibid.*, XVII, 493–97; Vaudreuil to Maurepas, November 2, 1748, *ibid.*, pp. 512–18.

28. Lanctot, *A History of Canada*, III, 74; Savelle, *The Diplomatic History of the Canadian Boundary*, pp. 45–46; Lionel Groulx, *Roland-Michel Barrin de la Galissonière 1693–1756* (Toronto: University of Toronto Press, 1970), p. 24. On some Indian attitudes towards European settlement and territorial encroachment see the Account of Mohawk conference with New York Council, *New York Colonial Documents*, VI, 870; Lawrence H. Gipson, *The British Empire before the American Revolution* (13 volumes. New York: Alfred A. Knopf, 1936–67), V, 64.

29. Beauharnois to Maurepas, October 9, 1744, *Wisconsin Historical Collections*, XVII, 441; Maurepas to La Galissonière, February 23, 1748, *ibid.*, XVIII, 12.

30. Rouillé held office from April 26, 1749, until July 28, 1754.

31. Stanley, *New France*, p. 36.

32. Rouillé to La Jonquière, May 4, 1749, *Wisconsin Historical Collections*, XVIII, 22–23.

33. Rouillé to La Jonquière and Bigot, May 4, 1749, *ibid.*, pp. 27–28.

34. La Galissonière to Rouillé, June 26, 1749, *Illinois Historical Collections*, XXIX, 97.

35. La Jonquière to Rouillé, September 30, 1750, *Wisconsin Historical Collections*, XVIII, 69. See also Céloron's own conclusions in his "Journal," *ibid.*, pp. 57–58.

36. Commandant at Fort Chartres to de Raymond, February 11, 1750, *ibid.*, p. 58; Ministerial Minutes on Despatches from Louisiana, September 18, 1750, *New York Colonial Documents*, X, 219–20.

37. Rouillé to La Jonquière, May 4, 1749, *Wisconsin Historical Collections*, XVIII, 21.

38. *Ibid.*, p. 24.

39. Ministerial Minutes on the Attempts of the English to Settle on the Ohio, September 23, 1751, *New York Colonial Documents*, X, 239.

40. The Indians preferred easy access to trading posts to driving the Anglo-Americans from their land. See Eccles, *The Canadian Frontier*, p. 159. Rouillé's perception of events was probably colored by La Galissonière who had returned to France in 1749 and had immediately begun to prepare a study on the situation in North America. This memoir owed much to his earlier report. Compare the two, *Wisconsin Historical Collections*, XVII, 493–97 and *New York Colonial Documents*, X, 222–30.

41. Conference of La Jonquière with the Cayuga, May 15, 1750, *New York Colonial Documents*, X, 207.

42. Eccles, *The Canadian Frontier*, p. 159.

43. Longueuil to Rouillé, April 21, 1759, *Wisconsin Historical Collections*, XVIII, 109–15.

44. Gipson, *The British Empire before the American Revolution*, V, 106–107.

45. *Ibid.*, pp. 29–31.

46. *Ibid.*, p. 107. See also Ministerial Minutes, September 23, 1751, *New York Colonial Documents*, X, 239; Longueuil to Rouillé, April 21, 1752, *Wisconsin Historical Collections*, XVIII, 107; La Jonquière to Céloron, October 29, 1751, *Illinois Historical Collections*, XXIX, 381–82, 387.

47. Duquesne was appointed in March, 1752, received his instructions in May, and did not arrive in New France until July. Lanctot, *A History of Canada*, III, 83–89; Duquesne's Instructions, May 15, 1752, *Wisconsin Historical Collections*, XVIII, 118–22; Longueuil to Rouillé, April 21, 1752, *ibid.*, p. 104.

48. Longueuil to Rouillé, April 21, 1752, *Wisconsin Historical Collections*, XVIII, 117.

49. Eccles, *The Canadian Frontier*, p. 160; Longueuil to Rouillé, August 18, 1752, *Illinois Historical Collections*, XXIX, 652–53; Duquesne to Rouillé, October 25, 1752, *Wisconsin Historical Collections*, XVIII, 128–29; Longueuil to Rouillé, April 21, 1752, *ibid.*, p. 115.

50. Rouillé to Duquesne, May 15, 1752, *Wisconsin Historical Collections*, XVIII, 118–22; Rouillé to Duquesne, July 9, 1752, *Illinois Historical Collections*, XXIX, 648–51.

51. Stanley, *New France*, pp. 47–51; Eccles, *The Canadian Frontier*, pp. 160–62.

52. Eccles, *The Canadian Frontier*, pp. 160–62.

53. Eccles, *France in America*, p. 208.

54. Benjamin Franklin made this point in 1751. Quoted in Van Alstyne, *The Rising American Empire*, p. 20.

Britain and the Ohio Valley, 1760–1775:
The Search for Alternatives in a Revolutionary Era

JACK M. SOSIN

In the far-reaching wars between England and France dating from 1689 the emphasis had long been on European rather than American conflict. But the clash at mid-eighteenth century at the headwaters of the Ohio River and in Acadia marked a turning point for the thinking of British ministers. Following appeals from the provincial governments they committed Britain to waging a colonial and maritime war. The encroachments of the French would "endanger all the Northern colonies," the cabinet concluded, "and tend to the total Destruction thereof and their Trade." The American provinces "must not be abandon'd."[1] The initial goal during the conflict lay in securing a frontier to provide security for the colonies. But the victories of 1759, the fall of Montreal, and the capitulation of New France in 1760 made possible increased British demands. The French had been unable to achieve any offsetting gains in Europe. While opinions differed among the British ministers on the question of peace terms, some favored retaining all of Canada "as our Northern Colonies would never be quiet without it. . . ."[2]

Once the governments of Britain and France undertook concrete negotiations, however, the British ministry unanimously agreed to demand the cession of Canada. Although the boundaries of New France *vis à vis* Louisiana, were to be in contention, the general issue of Canada was decided almost at once. The cabinet *was* divided on the terms to be accorded the French, but the primary question was not between Canada and the West Indies, but whether to demand only the North American territories and thus accord the Bourbon foes a relatively easy peace or to insist on the West Indian conquests *as well* and thus prolong the war. Those favoring an early peace prevailed at a key cabinet meeting on April 30, 1762, when the Earl of Bute proposed that Britain restore Martinique

---

Jack M. Sosin, colonial British and American historian, is Professor of History, University of Nebraska.

60

and Guadeloupe. In order to "secure in perpetuity our northern conquests from all future chicane," the Mississippi River would serve as the boundary between British and Bourbon possessions in North America.[3]

Having acquired Canada and the interior in order to promote the security of the colonies, the British ministers then sought to preserve this goal by providing for an adequate defense establishment and regulating Indian relations. The course of the late war had highlighted the shortcomings of the traditional methods whereby each provincial government had been responsible for its own affairs. Co-operation had been purely voluntary. Before mid-eighteenth century no sustained challenge had tested the effectiveness of the traditional system. Although of long duration, conflict with the Bourbon powers had been sporadic and localized. Dependent on the whites for weapons and utensils, the Indians themselves were enmeshed in these conflicts. As a Wyandot told one British Indian agent, no tribe could exist without the support of a white nation. Consequently, the assistance of the natives during wartime depended to some extent on the ability to supply them with trade goods. New York's Indian secretary described the traffic with the natives as the foundation of the Indian alliance, "the chief Cement which binds us together," and the "first Principle of our whole System of Indian politics."[4] With the failure of the colonies to ratify the joint system of defense and Indian affairs proposed at the Albany Congress, at the outbreak of hostilities in 1755 the imperial government had appointed two officials to superintend political relations with the tribes. Commercial affairs still came within the purview of the separate colonial regimes. Unfortunately for the peace of the frontier and the progress of the struggle against the French, English traders had earned a reputation for defrauding the natives. Lieutenant Governor Robert Dinwiddie of Virginia complained that their malpractices were chiefly responsible for the desertion of the tribes from the English interest. Many knowledgeable officials in America agreed with him that a reformation of Indian affairs was essential. And as early as 1757 the Commissioners of Trade and Plantations concluded that "the only effectual method . . . will be to establish one general system under the sole direction of the crown. . . ."[5]

Another source of difficulty with the tribes—one further jeopardizing the stability of the frontier and the alliances so necessary for the conduct of the war—stemmed from white encroachments on Indian land. This pressure, warned the superintendent in the northern district, was driving the natives into the arms of the French.[6] Appreciating the danger, the governor of Pennsylvania and high-ranking officers of the British army took steps to reassure the braves. At several meetings held at Pittsburgh with representatives of the tribes from the Ohio Valley and the Great Lakes, Colonel Henry Bouquet and General Robert Monckton assured the Indians that they would not be deprived of their lands. The commander-in-chief, General Jeffrey Amherst, confirmed these pledges. By 1760 the military had established a temporary line along the crest of the mountains beyond which the whites could neither hunt nor settle. Despite the protests of land speculators and frontiersmen, the government in London supported the military. The tribesmen seemed to have ended hostilities, the Commissioners of Trade and Plantations remonstrated, "solely upon Our having engaged . . . not to Settle upon their hunting Grounds. . . ." Any attempt to settle on western waters, under these circumstances a "most dangerous Tendency," would provoke the Indians. Consequently, there was to be no occupying "any Lands upon the waters of the Ohio" until further notice.[7]

The participation of the provincial governments in the war effort had also raised problems. Some colonies, particularly those in the North, made substantial contributions in men and money, but whatever the political merits of the system of voluntary responses to British requisitions, inconvenience, delay, and inefficiency were entailed in operating through thirteen separate legislatures each imbued with a local outlook. During the conflict with the Cherokee (1759–1761) the governors of the southern provinces requested that British troops be used in the offensive against the Indians. Francis Fauquier of Virginia was convinced that "provincial Troops alone cannot Effectually finish this Affair. . . ."[8] When combined colonial British forces captured immediate objectives in North America, some colonial assemblies reduced or terminated their contributions. For them the war was over. With the capitulation of New France and the conclusion of peace, responsibilities still remained for the *British* forces: garrisoning the former French and Spanish provinces with their potentially subversive populations as well as the posts on the frontier and the former French posts along the Great Lakes and on the major rivers. Here the commanding officers were charged with maintaining good relations with the tribes and protecting them from any injustice. Under their surveillance, civilian traders were to adhere strictly to regulations for the conduct of the trade at the posts formulated by the superintendent, Sir William Johnson.[9]

Within a few months following the cessation of hostilities royal officials had completed a comprehensive program. All that remained was to give formal expression to their measures once the definitive treaty of peace legally transferred the territories to the British crown. The royal proclamation formulated during the spring and summer of 1763 as it related to North America simply incorporated the *ad hoc* measures already sanctioned and in operation for two years. These seemed all the more necessary with the uprising of the tribesmen in the Northwest and the laxness of the provincial governments in responding to calls for men to defend the frontiers when the British army mounted an offensive to retake the smaller posts which had fallen to surprise attack.[10]

The entire British program for stabilizing the frontier, garrisoning the Northwest, and regulating the Indian trade depended on adequate financing. But the measures imposed by the British government, 1764–1765, to help defray the cost, including stamp duties, led to rioting in the coastal cities and widespread resistance. These reactions had an immediate and continuing effect on British policy for the interior. Some colonial governors, fearing they would be unable to maintain order, inquired of the commander-in-chief about the possibility of employing royal troops. General Thomas Gage replied that aside from the constitutional objections, the troops were "at a great distance and a good deal Dispersed." Under the current disposition it would take time to collect them for duty on the seaboard and at the cost of "almost deserting the Posts in the upper country."[11] Already overextended, the western garrisons were to be depleted as the revolutionary drama on the seaboard intensified. In time the need to control the eastern centers loomed larger in the minds of British authorities than did the need to stabilize the frontier.[12]

Further developments more immediately jeopardized the tenuous imperial program. Just as some Americans challenged the right of Parliament to tax them, so some questioned the measures the royal government imposed to stabilize the frontier by redressing the grievances of the tribesmen. Several other factors complicated administration of the British program. Frontiersmen resented traders supplying the natives with weapons and ammunition, but unless the British were able to maintain the traffic, the Indians would turn to their rivals. Restricting the British traders to the posts under the scrutiny of the military gave an advantage to the French from the right bank of the Mississippi operating directly in the Indian villages.[13] A more immediate unsettling development lay in the threat posed by speculators and frontiersmen to the boundary. The temporary line set by the military during the war with the French reflected neither the actual state of settlement nor the respective claims of the tribes and the whites. Land speculators soon were covertly marking out tracts on the headwaters of the Ohio while scores of frontier families were openly pushing onto forbidden territory. General Gage considered the local governments too weak to prevent these encroachments, an assessment shared by Lieutenant Governor Fauquier of Virginia. The provincial authorities were "set at open Defiance" since they did not have sufficient strength to enforce order.[14] Gage reminded the executive of Pennsylvania that settlement on lands west of the mountains had been the "Chief Occasion" of the defection of the tribesmen. The governors of both Pennsylvania and Virginia issued proclamations requiring the squatters to remove, but to no avail. "Perhaps the leaving them to the Mercy of the Indians," Fauquier conjectured, "may be the best if not the only Way to restrain them." A more merciful method was employed; British troops from Fort Pitt evacuated the settlers from the headwaters of the Ohio.[15]

The repeal of the Stamp Act early in 1766 momentarily quieted the controversy on taxation, but it did nothing to solve the problem of financing military supervision of the West. The garrisons remained on the frontier and in the interior, but they constituted a monetary burden. To some the solution was obvious: either the Americans must contribute for the support of the army, or the British must reduce their commitment. The violent reaction to the Stamp Act had inclined some men, Gage and the secretary at war, Viscount Barrington, among them, to favor the latter alternative if only because they saw the need for an effective military force on the seaboard to thwart the challenge to the authority of the mother country.[16]

Early in 1767 western policy brought the political dispute over taxation once more into prominence in Westminster when the secretary at war in the Chatham administration brought into the House of Commons the estimated budget for the American forces, over £400,000. The extraordinary expenditures for the Indian departments and the remote forts in the interior were particularly heavy. To George Grenville, whose ministry two years previously had implemented the Stamp Act, it was absurd for Britain to pay for the defense and support of those who denied that she had any right to tax them. Grenville in the House of Commons and Barrington and Charles Townshend (chancellor of the exchequer) urged in the ministry that American expenses be reduced by evacuating the army from the interior and returning control (and thus the charge) of Indian affairs to the colonies, while imposing fresh import duties to aid in defraying the remaining costs.[17] Barrington and Townshend pressed for quick action. But the minister most directly responsible for the colonies was the Earl of Shelburne as secretary of state for the Southern Department. He sought to delay a decision. With no leadership or unity in the ministry, the secretary of state and the chancellor of the exchequer went their own ways. Townshend was able to push through Parliament a series of bills for collecting some revenue, but the new import duties were more symbolic than practical, totally inadequate to meet the needs of the military establishment in the West no matter how great the reduction in forces.

With the death of Townshend in September, 1767, Shelburne had a free hand; the ministry was disintegrating and he faced little opposition. Because of his political ties he was susceptible to an arrangement which would avoid the embarrassing question of parliamentary taxation. Moreover, from the time he entered office, Shelburne was the target of colonial lobbyists, land speculators who sought to have set aside the restriction on expansion and to canvass support for colonies in the Ohio Valley and at Detroit. Ultimately they supplied the rationalizations for his program, but the key to his motivation was the reduction of military expenditures and raising revenue by means other than parliamentary taxes, by quitrents, a form of traditional land taxes paid to the Crown. Chief among the lobbyists were Benjamin Franklin, William Franklin (governor of New Jersey), and the Philadelphia house of Baynton, Wharton, and Morgan, who, among others, were creditors of Pennsylvania traders who had suffered losses during the Indian uprising in 1763. As compensation they hoped to secure from the Iroquois a large tract of land on the upper Ohio. Sir William Johnson, superintendent for Indian affairs in the northern district, and his deputy, George Croghan, were brought into the venture. Initially the group had campaigned for a colony in the Illinois country, but in 1766, turning their attention to the left bank of the Ohio, the speculators launched a barrage of letters calculated to convince the Chatham ministry that a westward revision of the boundary line was necessary. Unless the administration sanctioned the new line, the Philadelphians stressed in writing Franklin, their spokesman in London, "The Indians cannot give us the land. . . ."[18]

Employing the arguments of the lobbyists in favor of westward expansion, Shelburne in September, 1767, presented to an almost defunct cabinet a seemingly plausible plan. He would extend the boundary westward to the Ohio, form two interior colonies, retain but a few of the major fortifications, and return control of Indian affairs to the provincial governments. Thus expenses would be greatly reduced while the settlers at Detroit and in the Illinois country would provision the remaining garrisons on the spot. In time the Indians of the region would either migrate westward or become what the Americans termed "Domestick."[19] This program was based on certain assumptions: that the warriors would not resist settlements made in their country; that the provincial governments were able adequately to manage Indian affairs; that both traders and frontiersmen would show restraint in dealing with the tribes; and that the settlers would pay quitrents for their lands. In accepting the views of colonial lobbyists and misconstruing the advice of royal officials in America, Shelburne and his aides were exercising poor judgment although the program they advocated would serve to relieve them temporarily of the politically embarrassing problem of financing the North American defense establishment.

Shelburne left office early the following year. The conduct of colonial affairs now fell to the Earl of Hillsborough in the newly created post of secretary of state for the American Department. He was counted among those who favored reducing expenses and relocating the army for service on the seaboard by reducing the British commitment in the West and returning control of Indian affairs to the American governments. Consequently under his aegis the Commissioners of Trade did not entirely reject the Shelburne program submitted the previous year. In their report of March 7, 1768, they called for a westward revision of the boundary line so that lands then contested between the Indians and the white settlers could be purchased from the tribesmen. The superintendents of Indian affairs, Sir William Johnson and John Stuart, had been negotiating as early as 1765 with the Indians for a revision of the temporary boundary established by the military and sanctioned by the Proclamation of 1763. The commissioners also expected that this revision would accommodate legitimate needs for expansion. But they rejected the proposals inspired by the speculators for colonies at Detroit and the Illinois country as impractical and likely to antagonize the tribesmen. Such settlements would require additional military protection and, located over a thousand miles from the sea by difficult river transportation, they could not be of economic consequence for Britain. Reflecting the thinking of those who had argued strongly for the need to reduce expenses, the commissioners further recommended that the provincial governments again manage commercial relations with the Indians. Presumably, having learned from experience, the Americans would recognize that a well-regulated trade was essential to their peace and security. Finally, the military should best decide the number and location of the forts in the interior required to maintain public safety and prevent incursions by the French and Spanish. Royal troops, not provincials, should garrison these posts.[20]

Hillsborough and Barrington pressed that the cabinet adopt this report and require the army to retain only three posts along the Great Lakes, Niagara, Detroit, and Michilimackinac. Since some ministers objected to what seemed an evacuation of the interior, a compromise formula was adopted by which the army would continue to garrison Fort Chartres or some other fortification in the Illinois country and its supply base at the Forks of the Ohio, as well as Crown Point or Ticonderoga to secure communications with Quebec. The commander-in-chief was allowed, however, to exercise his own judgment on all the posts except those on the Great Lakes. Barrington was quick to point out to Gage in their private correspondence that under this formula it was now within his power to evacuate the forts from the mountains down the Ohio to the Illinois country. As Hillsborough explained the adjustment in policy to the commander-in-chief, the ministry hoped to reduce expenses, preserve the unity and discipline of the forces so that they might be able to operate more effectively in an emergency, and mollify the Indians by offering the tribes compensation and a new boundary to alleviate their apprehensions.[21]

Subsequent developments in America threatened to undermine the revised program, especially the negotiations for the new boundary with the Indians. During talks with the Six Nations held at Fort Stanwix in the Mohawk country, Sir William Johnson deviated from his instructions in order to further the claims of certain land speculators, in particular the Philadelphia merchants and politicians who had succeeded to the claims of the traders suffering losses in the Indian raids of 1763. The Six Nations now granted them territory actually occupied by other tribes, a tract called "Indiana," bounded by Little Kanawha Creek, the Laurel Ridge, the Monongahela, and the southern boundary of Pennsylvania. Since this territory lay within the jurisdiction claimed by Virginia, as compensation Johnson allowed the southern terminus of the Indian boundary line to be extended down the Ohio from the mouth of the Great Kanawha to the mouth of the Tennessee. By Johnson's negotiations much of Kentucky was now open to the Virginians; they had been excluded from this region by the terms of the treaty negotiated by John Stuart, the superintendent for the southern district, with the Cherokee at Hard Labor, South Carolina. In seeking to justify his actions, Johnson claimed to the home government that he could not deny the right of the Iroquois, the stronger of the two Indian groups, to make the grant to the traders or to claim the left bank of the Ohio as far as the Tennessee without endangering the entire negotiation. In London the secretary of state was reluctant to accept the revisions as they threatened to embroil the British with the Cherokee and other tribes and seemed to have been contrived simply to benefit private interests. Particularly objectionable was the supposed insistence of the Iroquois that the grant to the Pennsylvania traders be a condition for the entire negotiation at Fort Stanwix.[22]

In order to secure confirmation of the grant, the Philadelphia syndicate in the spring of 1769 sent two agents, William Trent and Samuel Wharton, to London. The son of a Quaker merchant, Wharton was possibly one of the least scrupulous, but most effective manipulators of his day. He achieved remarkable success in building up a lobby of almost unprecedented proportions. Not only was he able to nullify the opposition of spokesmen for rival Virginia speculators, he was also able to involve high-ranking politicians both within and without the Grafton-North administration in a massive land speculating scheme. The group came to be called the Walpole Associates after Wharton's principal ally, the London banker Thomas Walpole. Wharton and his partners eventually sought to secure a patent for a fourteenth colony, Vandalia, a joint proprietary venture for an interior province encompassing much of the land ceded at Fort Stanwix and extending roughly from the forks of the Ohio to the Kentucky River and bounded on the east by the Appalachian Mountains. They aimed at acquiring this tract, variously estimated to include from twenty to forty million acres, for the sum the Crown had paid to the Six Nations at Fort Stanwix, some £10,000. By referring the matter to officials in Virginia and the Penn family, Hillsborough and his allies on the Board of Trade were able to defer any decision for over two years. By this time news from America made it clear that the western and southern tribesmen resented the sale by the Six Nations, thus confirming for Hillsborough his apprehensions over the recent boundary negotiations. They seemed to have no other effect than extending the settlements and provoking an Indian war.[23] But Hillsborough had few supporters in London. Many in the inner circle of government may have opposed him to further their financial interest in the Walpole Associates, or simply to eliminate the chief supporter of Lord North whom they sought to oust from office. Whatever the case, leading members of the council united in rejecting a report unfavorable to the projected new colony. Hillsborough resigned over the issue and was replaced in August, 1772, by the more compliant Earl of Dartmouth.

Yet the bureaucratic machinery was slow in processing the patent for Vandalia. Hillsborough's allies, the Crown law officers, further delayed matters by throwing up technical objections to certain legal aspects of the grant. More than a year passed and time had run out on the speculators. The drama of the American Revolution was about to open and Samuel Adams and his Boston "Mohawks" raised the curtain on the night of December 16, 1773. In recounting the reception given the tea ships in America, one of the Philadelphia Whartons hoped that by this time "the business of Vandalia is Completed," for if not, given the situation in America, their opponents would "have fresh Vigor" to oppose the project.[24]

Events on the turbulent frontier as well as in the coastal cities had overtaken the speculators in London. Several days before the episode in Boston, the secretary of state revealed that the British government was about to embark on a new policy for the Northwest. The inertia of the provincial assemblies in regulating Indian affairs was in part responsible. Two years after control over commercial relations with the tribes had been restored to the colonies, the provinces still had not acted. Several governors, not overly sanguine, agreed to send delegates to a congress where they might draft a general plan of regulation. Cognizant of the use to which a congress had been put during the crisis over the Stamp Act, Hillsborough had refused to permit the governors to send commissioners. He was not unaware of the difficulty entailed in drafting a general scheme for the trade while depending on the concurrence of several colonies, each with diverse interests. This was not the only instance to demonstrate the necessity of a "general superintending Power over all the British Dominion in America," an authority the colonists had unhappily resisted. The secretary of state urged the superintendents to frame a law to be recommended to the respective colonial legislatures.[25] But no action was forthcoming and many of the governors joined the superintendents in criticizing the negligence of the local assemblies. The inability of the commanders of the posts in the interior to prevent the traders from traveling among the Indian villages made the situation all the more difficult. Describing the traders in general as "the outcasts of all Nations, and the refuse of Mankind," Major Henry Basset at Detroit would have liked sufficient police power as "to make these Vagabonds tremble. . . ." The military could take no action without the traders raising the cry of "English Liberty" and threatening to sue in the civil courts of the seaboard provinces. The commandants did not even have sufficient authority to send violators to New York or Quebec for trial.[26] The irregular methods employed by the traders brought the strongest complaints as the tempers of the tribesmen mounted. By 1773 the new secretary of state, fully appreciating that the provinces did "not seem disposed" to concur in any general regulatory scheme, professed himself "at a Loss to suggest any Mode" for maintaining the Indian service other than by the "interposition of the Authority of the supreme Legislature."[27]

The decision by the commander-in-chief to evacuate additional garrisons further weakened imperial authority in the interior. Fort Chartres in the Illinois country and its supply base at Fort Pitt alone accounted for more than half of the expenses of the Indian department in the northern district. So perplexed was Gage over the problems of the interior and the French inhabitants that he wrote privately: "I wish most sincerely that there was neither Settler nor Soldier in any part of the Indian country" and that the British were free of both the trouble and expense. With the post on the Mississippi rapidly decaying, the cabinet finally agreed that Gage could evacuate Fort Chartres and Fort Pitt, and submit a plan "on the lowest plan of Expense" for a civil establishment for the French inhabitants in the Wabash and Illinois valleys.[28] The decision to abandon "two such expensive and troublesome Posts" afforded the commander-in-chief great pleasure. If the colonists forced the Indians into war "by using them ill, let them feel the Consequences, we shall be out of the Scrape," he confided to the secretary at war.[29] By the end of 1772 only a temporary, token force of fifty soldiers remained at Kaskaskia while the royal army had withdrawn completely from Fort Pitt. In the ensuing year a three-cornered struggle developed for control of the forks of the Ohio among the supporters of Vandalia, the adherents of Pennsylvania, and the proponents of Virginia. Across the Ohio the tribesmen grew more and more apprehensive.

With the situation in America deteriorating the British government in 1773 once more sought to intervene. It acted first to rectify the disorderly system of disposing of land. New regulations drafted that year were incorporated early in 1774 in the instructions issued to royal governors. Surveys designated on maps must precede actual grants. The governors were to have land auctioned off in small lots to the highest bidder at publicly stipulated times and places with at least four months' prior notice.[30] At the same time the ministry turned its attention to the Indian trade and the French settlers in the Illinois country, along the Wabash and at Detroit. During the British occupation these settlers had been under military jurisdiction. Two developments made the situation acute: speculators began to make unauthorized purchases from some Indians of large tracts of land occupied by other tribes in the Illinois and Wabash valleys, and the settlers put strong pressure on the authorities to grant them civil government.

Given the failure of the program of accommodation instituted five years before, by the end of 1773, even before the crisis with Massachusetts reached a peak, the North ministry had decided to extend jurisdiction through the province of Quebec, the only colony to demonstrate in the past decade some ability to deal with the tribesmen.[31] By the terms of the Quebec Act, passed in the spring of 1774, the boundaries of Quebec were extended to include the region north of the Ohio and east of the Mississippi rivers. Early the following year the Privy Council instructed the governor of Quebec to adopt regulations for the conduct of the Indian trade developed a decade before by the royal superintendents.[32] Constrained by financial and military exigencies and the failure of previous solutions, the ministry saw the Quebec Act as the only effective alternative. It represented an honest attempt to insure the stability of the Northwest. Flagrant encroachments on Indian lands had antagonized the tribes already dissatisfied with the chaotic state of the trade. They were thought to be forming a confederacy, and a general Indian war seemed in the offing.

Many of the warriors had disapproved of the extensive cessions of land but were tempted by the presents they had been offered. The younger, more warlike braves were particularly concerned over the loss of their immediate hunting grounds.[33] The very technique of negotiating cession often led to dissatisfaction. White authorities found it expedient to bargain with one group for lands claimed or occupied by another tribe. In June, 1773, some Cherokee indebted to white traders ceded to Georgia over two million acres claimed by the Lower Creeks. Along the Ohio, the Mingo, Shawnee, and Delawares, displaced from their lands by the treaty signed with the Six Nations, complained bitterly to the tribes around the Great Lakes that the Iroquois had left them without hunting grounds. They threatened to resist if the whites took possession.

Killbuck, the Delaware chief, warned at Fort Pitt in December, 1771: "Black Clouds begin to gather fast in this Country."[34] More disturbing reports now reached the superintendents of Indian affairs. Tribes traditionally hostile to each other appeared ready to put aside their differences and to unite against the whites. The Creeks appealed to the Chickasaw to mediate a peace with the Choctaw, and with the Shawnee and Ottawa they called on the Cherokee to unite. A mission of young Cherokee traveled north to negotiate peace among the different tribes, and particularly to resolve the feud with the Six Nations. Early in 1774 delegates from the Mingo and Delawares conferred on the Scioto with emissaries of the Overhill Cherokee on means to resist aggression by the whites. Intertribal war was to cease and a united front was to be presented to the common enemy. It was better for the Indians to unite and resist now though death and defeat might follow. The whites would destroy them in any case, and the warrior's death was better than gradual extermination.[35]

It was ominous for the frontier settlements that the Overhill Cherokee and the Shawnee played leading roles in these negotiations, for these tribes were directly involved in efforts by the frontiersmen and land speculators to penetrate into Kentucky by way of the Ohio River and overland through the Cumberland Gap. It was the boast of the expansionist governor of Virginia, Lord Dunmore, who sought to force the Indians to accept white occupation of the left bank of the Upper Ohio, that notwithstanding "all the tribes of the south and west are joined," the Virginia forces would "give a pretty good account" of themselves.[36] When Dunmore marched against the Indians in the fall of 1774, the exposed settlements he left behind on the frontier were not attacked; and the Virginians were able to enjoy great numerical superiority on the Ohio because officials of the British Indian department neutralized the other tribes and thus isolated the Shawnee and Delawares. Guy Johnson, who had succeeded his uncle as superintendent in the northern district, prevailed on the Iroquois to send emissaries to the western Wyandots, Hurons, and Ottawa to offset the plea of the Shawnee. To the south John Stuart dispatched his deputies to manage the Choctaw and to hinder the Chickasaw from mediating between the southern tribes. The Cherokee, kept short of ammunition and unable to reach an accommodation with the Creeks, did not attack the exposed Virginia frontier. The Creeks were themselves menaced by the hostile Choctaw at their backs. Thus the Shawnee and Delawares were isolated on the Ohio.[37] The success of the British Indian department in disrupting the Indian coalition was not without irony and significance for the future. During the Revolutionary War when they were called on to bring in the tribesmen against the rebellious colonists, the superintendents were never fully able to repair the damage wrought by their diplomacy during Dunmore's War.

British policy for the Northwest had been formulated while bulk transportation was limited to watercraft powered by wind, current, and muscle, and before the technological revolution of the nineteenth century—the application of steam to transportation—made economic exploitation of the North American interior possible. Faced with similar limitations and confronted with comparable problems, the American Congress after independence was to adopt a policy exhibiting the same characteristics—central management of Indian affairs, restraints on encroachments on Indian territory, and orderly disposal of land. It was to be equally unsuccessful.

NOTES

1. See the memorandum of the cabinet meeting, June 26, 1754, London, British Museum, Newcastle Papers, Add. MSS 33029, f.124; the Duke of Newcastle to Horatio Walpole, June 29, 1754, *ibid.*, Add. MSS 32735, f.597. See also Richard Pares, "American *versus* Continental Warfare, 1739–1763," in *English Historical Review*, LI(1936), 429–65, and Thad W. Riker, "The Politics behind Braddock's Expedition," in *American Historical Review*, XIII (1908), 742–52.

2. Newcastle to the Earl of Hardwicke, December 3, 1760, Newcastle Papers, Add. MSS 32915, ff.270–71; Hardwicke to Newcastle, March 17, 1761, *ibid.*, Add. MSS 32920, f.271; and Newcastle to Hardwicke, April 17, 1761, *ibid.*, Add. MSS 32923, f.19.

3. Newcastle to Hardwicke, April 25, 1762, Newcastle Papers, Add. MSS 32937, f.349; same to same, May 1, 1762, *ibid.*, Add. MSS 32938, f.10; and Bute to the Duke of Bedford (British plenipotentiary at Versailles), May 1, 1762, in *Correspondence of John, 4th Duke of Bedford* (3 volumes. London, 1842–46), III, 74–75. When news reached London of the capture of Havana, the ministers on October 22, decided to insist either on Florida or Puerto Rico as restitution for the return of the Cuban city. The Earl of Egremont to Bedford, October 26, 1762, *ibid.*, III, 139. The Spanish chose to relinquish Florida and were in turn compensated by the French with the cession of Louisiana west of the Mississippi River. Following the signing of the preliminary treaty of Paris on November 3, 1762, the British Parliament voted on the proposed terms. By this time such key politicians as Newcastle and William Pitt were no longer in office. While they attacked certain portions of the peace treaty, Parliament approved of the provisions relating to North America. On the entire question of British motives and the negotiations leading up to the peace of Paris of 1763, see Jack M. Sosin, *Whitehall and the Wilderness: The Middle West in British Colonial Policy, 1760–1775* (Lincoln: University of Nebraska Press, 1961), pp. 5–25.

4. Nicholas B. Wainwright (ed.), "George Croghan's Journal, 1759–1763," in *Pennsylvania Magazine of History and Biography*, LXXI (1947), 357; Peter Wraxall, *An Abridgment of Indian Affairs . . . in the Colony of New York . . .*, edited by Charles H. McIlwain (*Harvard Historical Studies*, No. 21. Cambridge, Mass., 1915), p. 153.

5. Dinwiddie to the Commissioners of Trade, February 23, 1756, in Robert A. Brock (ed.), *The Official Records of Robert Dinwiddie . . . 1751–1758 (Virginia*

Historical Collections, 2 volumes. Richmond, Va., 1882–92), II, 338–39; Wilbur R. Jacobs (ed.), *The Edmund Atkin Report and Plan of 1755* (Columbia: University of South Carolina Press, 1954), pp. 3, 8, 17–18, 40; "Sketch of a System for the Management of Indian Affairs in North America under One General Direction," in Charles H. Lincoln (ed.), *Correspondence of William Shirley Governor of Massachusetts and Military Commander in America, 1731–1760* (2 volumes. New York: The Macmillan Co., 1912), II, 373–77; George Washington to Francis Fauquier, December 2, 1758, in John C. Fitzpatrick (ed.), *The Writings of George Washington* (39 volumes. Washington, D.C.: U.S. Government Printing Office, 1931–44), II, 313–14; Sir William Johnson to Gen. Jeffrey Amherst, December 8, 1759, in James Sullivan *et al.* (eds.), *The Papers of Sir William Johnson* (16 volumes. Albany and New York, 1921–60), III, 183 (hereafter cited as *Johnson Papers*); and the Commissioners of Trade to Gov. Henry Littleton of South Carolina, November 9, 1757, London, Public Record Office, C.O. 5/403/201–203.

6. William West to Thomas Penn, January 12, 1756, Loudoun Papers, LO 757, Henry E. Huntington Library, San Marino, California; Johnson to Amherst, September 18, 1759, *Johnson Papers*, III, 138; Johnson to the Commissioners of Trade, September 10, May 28, November 10, 1756, May 17, 1759 in Edmund B. O'Callaghan (ed.), *Documents Relative to the Colonial History of the State of New York* (15 volumes. Albany, N.Y., 1856–87), VII, 87, 170, 377 (hereafter cited as *New York Colonial Documents*).

7. See the proceedings of various meetings with the tribes in Colonial Records of Pennsylvania, *Minutes of the Provincial Council,* 1683–1776 (10 volumes. Philadelphia, 1852–53), VIII, 199; Samuel Hazard *et al.* (eds.), *Pennsylvania Archives* (9 series, 138 volumes. Philadelphia and Harrisburg, 1852–1949), 1st series, III, 572, 745, IV, 49; Commissioners of Trade to Fauquier of Virginia, June 13, 1760, C.O. 5/1367/409–12, and same to same, February 17, 1761, C.O. 5/1368/12–15.

8. Fauquier to Gen. Jeffrey Amherst, December 13, 1760, in H. R. McIlwaine and J. P. Kennedy (eds.), *Journals of the House of Burgesses of Virginia (1619–1776)* (13 volumes. Richmond, Va.: 1905–15), 1758–1761, p. 267. For a discussion of the difficulties in the requisition system see Sosin, *Whitehall and the Wilderness,* pp. 33–36, and especially Douglas E. Leach, *Arms for Empire, A Military History of the British Colonies in North America, 1607–1763* (New York: Macmillan, 1973).

9. See Amherst to Johnson, June 24, 1761, *Johnson Papers*, III, 422–23; Johnson to Col. Henry Bouquet, September 18, 1761, *ibid.,* III, 529; and Johnson's regulations for the Indian trade, *ibid.,* III, 527–28.

10. When the new commander-in-chief of the British forces in America, Gen. Thomas Gage, called on the governments of the middle and northern colonies to provide men, New York and New Jersey agreed to provide but half the number requested. Provincial troops were thought to be unreliable. Col. Henry Bouquet who was to lead one of the columns into the Indian country noted that of the 950 men sent by Pennsylvania, 200 had deserted before operations had begun. The provincials continued to desert even on the march, taking horses and arms with them. He swore that he would never again "depend upon new[ly] raised troops," Bouquet to Lt. Gov. John Penn, August 22, 1764, *Pennsylvania Archives,* 1st series, IV, 206; Bouquet to Gage, September 5, 1764, *Michigan Pioneer and Historical Collections,* XIX(1891), 273.

11. Gage to Cadwallader Colden, lieutenant governor of New York, August 31, 1765, in *The Letters and Papers of Cadwallader Colden,* VII, 1765–1775 (New-York Historical Society *Collections,* LVI, New York, 1923), pp. 57–58; and Gage to Francis Bernard, September 25, 1765, in Edward Channing and Archibald C.

Coolidge (eds.), *Barrington-Bernard Correspondence (Harvard Historical Studies,* No. 17, Cambridge, Mass., 1912), p. 230.

12. The initial disposition of the military forces in North America following the capitulation of the French had left the garrisons widely scattered and divided over a vast continent so that in Gage's words, "Very few could be collected in case of sudden Emergencies" except in Canada. In the spring of 1766 the commander-in-chief began what was to be merely the first of several modifications; the evacuation of several of the smaller posts while leaving such garrisons as were absolutely necessary for the larger installations. Before he had not been able to gather even two companies for an emergency; now he expected to assemble a corps equal to three regiments. Gage to Secretary of State Henry Conway, September 23, 1765, in Clarence W. Alvord and Clarence E. Carter (eds.), *The New Regime, 1765-1767 (Illinois Historical Collections,* XI, Springfield, Ill., 1916), p. 87; Gage to Viscount Barrington, March 29, 1766, in Clarence E. Carter (ed.), *The Correspondence of General Thomas Gage* (2 volumes. New Haven: Yale University Press, 1931-33), II, 345; and Gage to Conway, May 6, 1766, *ibid.,* I, 90.

13. Gage to Penn, June 16, 1765, *Minutes of the Provincial Council of Pennsylvania,* IX, 268.

14. Gage to Johnson, May 5, 1766, *Johnson Papers,* V, 201; Fauquier to the Earl of Halifax, June 14, 1766, C.O. 5/1345/159-60.

15. Fauquier to the Commissioners of Trade and Plantations, July 26, 1766, C.O. 5/1331/306; Gage to Gov. John Penn, July 2, 1766, *Minutes of the Provincial Council of Pennsylvania,* IX, 321-22; Fauquier to Penn, December 11, 1766, *ibid.,* IX, 349; and Gage to Penn, December 7, 1766, *ibid.,* IX, 403.

16. On the thinking of Barrington and Gage see their private correspondence from October, 1765, to October, 1768, in the Gage Papers, William L. Clements Library, University of Michigan, Ann Arbor.

17. On the debates in the House of Commons of January 26 and February 18, 1767, and the cabinet discussions of March 12 and March 30, 1767, see William Samuel Johnson to William Pitkin, February 12, 1767, Massachusetts Historical Society, *Collections,* 5th series, IX (Boston, 1885), 215-16; Grenville to the Earl of Buckingham, January 27, 1767, Grenville Letterbook, Stowe Collection, St. 7, Huntington Library; Lord George Sackville to John Irwin, February 13, 1767, in Historical Manuscripts Commission, *Report on the Manuscripts of Mrs. Stopford-Sackville . . .* (2 volumes. London, 1904), I, 119; William Rouet to Baron Mure, January 21, 1767, in William Mure (ed.), *Caldwell Family Papers . . . (Maitland Club Publications.* 2 volumes in 3 parts. Glasgow, 1854), II, Pt. 2, pp. 101, 106-108; the Earl of Shelburne to the Earl of Chatham, February 1, March 13, 1767, the Duke of Grafton to Chatham, March 13, 1767, in W. S. Taylor and J. H. Pringle (eds.), *Correspondence of William Pitt, Earl of Chatham* (4 volumes. London, 1838-40), III, 184-85, 231, 232-33; Barrington to Gage (private), February 10, March 13, 1767, Gage Papers; and William Samuel Johnson to Jared Ingersoll (private), February 28, 1766 [1767], William Samuel Johnson Papers, Letters by, 1767-92 (2), Connecticut Historical Society, Hartford.

18. Baynton, Wharton, and Morgan to Franklin, August 28, 1766, Franklin Papers, Misc. I, 54-55, Library of Congress, Washington, D.C.

19. "Minutes submitted to the Cabinet the beginning [*sic*] of [the] Summer [of] 1767 relative to the System of Indian traffick . . . ," Shelburne Papers, Clements Library, X, 185-217. The heading was written in later which probably accounts for the mistaken reference to the early summer of 1767. The paper was actually presented to the cabinet on September 11, 1767. See Shelburne's minute of the meeting of that date, *ibid.,* CLXI, unfoliated.

20. This report, March 7, 1768 (misdated March 17), is printed in *New York Colonial Documents*, VIII, 19–31.

21. Barrington to Gage (private), March 12, April 4, 1768, Gage Papers; minute of cabinet, March 18, 1768, C.O. 5/1008/146; and Hillsborough to Gage, April 15, 1768, in Carter (ed.), *Correspondence of General Gage*, II, 64.

22. Johnson to Hillsborough, November 18, 1768, *New York Colonial Documents*, VIII, 110. Denied any co-operation by the Virginians, Stuart had concluded an agreement with the Cherokee which set the boundary between them and Virginia at a line running from Chiswell's Mines on a branch of the lower Kanawha northwest to the confluence of the Kanawha and the Ohio. By the unauthorized action of Johnson, however, the Virginians could now claim the right to expand into Kentucky on the basis of a cession by the Iroquois and thus ignore the rights of the Cherokee. Stuart was forced to renegotiate the boundary with the Cherokee at Lochaber in 1770. While the evidence is not quite conclusive, it strongly indicates that Johnson, now involved with the land speculators, extended the northern line down the Ohio to obtain Virginia's acquiescence to the grant for the Philadelphia speculators in a district over which the southern colony claimed jurisdiction. For the very complicated story of these negotiations see Sosin, *Whitehall and the Wilderness*, pp. 169–80.

23. Johnson to Hillsborough, January 6, 1770, *Johnson Papers*, VII, 332; George Croghan to Johnson, December 22, 1769, *ibid.*, VII, 316; John Stuart to Hillsborough, April 27, 1771, C.O. 5/72/421; and Hillsborough to Johnson, July 1, 1772, *Johnson Papers*, VIII, 302.

24. Thomas Wharton to Thomas Walpole, December 21, 1773, Wharton Letterbook, 1773–84, Historical Society of Pennsylvania, Philadelphia. On the Vandalia episode see Sosin, *Whitehall and the Wilderness*, pp. 181–210.

25. Hillsborough to Lt. Gov. Colden of New York, April 14, 1770, *New York Colonial Documents*, VIII, 210; Colden to Governor Botetourt of Virginia, April 16, 1770, C.O. 5/1349/117; Botetourt to Lt. Gov. John Penn of Pennsylvania, June 17, 1770, *Pennsylvania Archives*, 1st series, IV, 317; Gov. Guy Carleton of Quebec to Colden, May 30, 1770, C.O. 5/1349/153; Colden to Hillsborough, July 7, 1770, *New York Colonial Documents*, VIII, 216; Johnson to Hillsborough, August 14, 1770, *ibid.*, VIII, 225; Hillsborough to the colonial governors (circular), November 11, 1770, C.O. 5/71/441–44; and Hillsborough to John Stuart, July 3, 1771, C.O. 5/72/482–83.

26. See Maj. Henry Basset to Gen. Frederick Haldimand, April 29, 1773, *Michigan Pioneer and Historical Collections*, XIX (1891), 298–99.

27. Dartmouth to Sir William Johnson, February 3, 1773, C.O. 5/74/29ff.

28. Gage to Gen. Frederick Haldimand, June 27, 1768, London, British Museum, Haldimand Papers, Add. MSS, 21663, f. 297; Gage to Johnson, April 4, August 7, 1768, *Johnson Papers*, VII, 177, 313; Gage to Hillsborough, June 16, 1768, and Hillsborough to Gage, December 4, 1771, in Carter (ed.), *Correspondence of General Gage*, I, 175–79, II, 137; Gage to Barrington (private), November 1, 1770, Gage Papers.

29. Gage to Barrington, March 4, 1772, in Carter (ed.), *Correspondence of General Gage*, II, 601.

30. See the draft of additional instructions to the governors dated June 3, 1773, C.O. 324/18/45–62; and the circular letter from the Secretary of State, February 5, 1774, C.O. 5/75/53–54. The instructions to the governor of New York are printed in *New York Colonial Documents*, VIII, 410–12.

31. On this decision see Jack M. Sosin, "The French Settlements in British Policy for the North American Interior, 1760–1774," in *Canadian Historical Review*,

XXXIX (1958), 199–208. The Boston Tea Party occurred on the night of December 16, 1773. On December 1, the secretary of state for the American Department wrote to a representative of the French settlers in the Illinois country confirming that some form of government was necessary for the Illinois, although he did not think a government independent of any other colony could be appropriate. Dartmouth to Daniel Blouin, December 1, 1773, C.O. 5/74/361. That same day he wrote to the lieutenant governor of Quebec, the former French province whose limits had been reduced by the Proclamation of 1763, that the policy on which that edict had been founded could no longer be maintained and that the propriety of restricting the colony to the narrow limits prescribed by the proclamation was subject to doubt. Dartmouth to Hector Cramahé, December 1, 1773, C.O. 42/32/93–94.

32. See articles 31 and 32 of the additional instructions to Gov. Guy Carleton, in Adam Shortt and Arthur Doughty (eds.), *Documents Relating to the Constitutional History of Canada, 1759–1791* (Ottawa, 1907), p. 428.

33. John Stuart to Gage, December 14, 1771, and Alexander Cameron to Stuart, March 9, 1771, enclosed in Stuart to Gage, April 29, 1771, Gage Papers.

34. See the report of his speech in the Gage Papers for that year; also George Croghan to Gage, January 1, 1770, *ibid.*, and Johnson to Hillsborough, January 6, 1770, April 4, 1772, *Johnson Papers*, VII, 332, VIII, 292.

35. For information on these attempts to unite the tribes see Charles Edmonstone to Gage, April 24, 1771, and John Stuart to Gage, December 14, 1771, Gage Papers; Stuart to Gen. Frederick Haldimand, February 3, 1774, transcripts of Haldimand Papers, XII, 263, Public Archives of Canada, Ottawa; Edward Wilkinson to Alexander Cameron, enclosed in Stuart to Gage, August 8, 1774, Capt. Arent Depeyster to Haldimand, July 16, 1774, and Alexander Cameron to Stuart, June 17, 1774, in Stuart to Gage, July 3, 1774, all in Gage Papers.

36. Dunmore to Gage, June 11, 1774, Gage Papers.

37. On the role of the superintendents see Guy Johnson to Gage, July 12, August 11, 19, September 29, 1774, *ibid.*; Johnson to Penn, July 22, 1774, in Peter Force (ed.), *American Archives* (Series 4 and 5, 9 volumes. Washington, D.C., 1837–53), 4th series, I, 645–46; Johnson to Dartmouth, September 10, 1774, *New York Colonial Documents*, VIII, 490; Stuart to Haldimand, June 25, 1774, and Stuart to Gage, May 12, November 19, 1774, Gage Papers; and Stuart to Haldimand, November 20, 1774, transcripts of Haldimand Papers, XII, 397. For a fuller discussion of this incident and subsequent attempts to use the Indians see Jack M. Sosin, "The British Indian Department and Dunmore's War," in *Virginia Magazine of History and Biography*, LXXIV (1966), 34–50, and "The Use of Indians in the War of the American Revolution: A Re-Assessment of Responsibility," in *Canadian Historical Review*, XLVI (1965), 101–21.

The Advance of the Anglo-American Frontier, 1700–1783

Thomas D. Clark

Historians of the Anglo-American frontier have often revealed a degree of indecision as to the time and place when the westward movement began. It began with the landing of the first immigrants at the various points of penetration along the Atlantic Coast, and within the roar of the lapping tides of the Chesapeake Bay and James River estuaries. Simultaneously there began the process of American pioneering which underwent refinements as each new frontier was opened. By this term is implied the act of European adaptations not only to new and somewhat strange geographic and climatic environments, but likewise adjusting to exploitation of a generous category of new raw materials, the establishment of a different and basic routine of daily social and economic life, and of learning to live with a possible Indian menace on the outer fringe of every new settlement.[1]

Of utmost significance was the fact that there was present along the rugged foreseam of that portion of the American continent from the Atlantic to the Mississippi the raw materials in somewhat readily available form for sustaining a dynamic era of pioneering. To the west lay an unbounded mass of virgin land which on its very face promised almost unlimited production of basic materials not only for expanding an elementary human society but for creating a rich continental commercial and speculative system.[2]

John Smith sensed this from his severely limited perspective at Jamestown. He wrote, "The mildness of the ayr, the fertilitie of the soyle, and situation of the rivers are so propitious to the nature and use of man, as no place is more convenient for pleasure, profit, and man's sustenance, under that latitude or climat. Here will live any beasts, as horses, goats, sheepe, asses, hens, &c. as appeared by them that were

---

Thomas D. Clark, historian of colonial and frontier America, is Professor Emeritus of History, Indiana University.

77

carried thether. The waters, Isles, and shoales, are full of safe harbours for ships of warre or merchandize, for boats of all sorts, for transportation of fishing &c."[3]

From the outset the Anglo-American backwoods settler approached the great wooded hinterland with certainty that potential danger lurked in every quarter. From the Susquehanna to the upper reaches of the Tennessee; along the Shenandoah, the James, the Greenbriar, the Holston, the Clinch, and subsequently the Kanawha and the Kentucky, the land was in constant turmoil over the competition between settler and Indian.[4] Persistently the Anglo settler moved westward establishing his combination line of lonely cabins and puncheon fortresses. The latter were crude log bastions, sometimes no more than solidly built log houses.[5] Whatever their type of construction or design they resembled the formal European stronghold only in general defense purpose, and certainly not in human occupation or usage.[6] It is a remarkable fact in eighteenth-century American frontier history that very few of these fortifications were taken by the Indians; the most notable exceptions were Ruddles' and Hinkston's forts on the Licking River in central Kentucky.[7]

Like so many backwoods enterprises, the presence of the fort represented a common community facility and responsibility, and its defense was the duty of those using it.[8] In a majority of cases the appearance of these central defensive posts symbolized two major facts of western expansion: the outer fringes of the settlement line had expanded that far, and settlers established the point indelibly that they had come to stay. More than a century and a quarter elapsed between the location of the Abraham Woods Fort on the James River, and the neighboring ones at the Falls of the York and of the Appomattox, and the building of Harrod's and Boone's fortresses in Kentucky.[9] In between, and over a geographical space of approximately five hundred miles, other major fortresses came to form landmarks of Anglo expansion. Among these were Cumberland, Winchester (Fort Loudoun), Pitt, Watauga, and Loudon on the Hiawasse in eastern Tennessee.[10] These were classic representatives of both frontier fortification and staging posts for the westward advancing settlers.

Both the defense and the human thrust of the Anglo frontier developed need for an informal plan of defense which in time was to form the foundational tradition of the military system of the American republic itself.[11] From the outset of the westward movement in from the Atlantic the defense of the raw outer limits of the settlement line was as much an individual responsibility as participation in the domestic common workings of cabin raisings, logrollings, and quiltings. Wherever along the colonial frontier citizens were involved in defense they selected their officers, participated in making plans of strategy, helped supply arms and materials, skirmished, and shared the fruits of victory or the dregs of defeat. Whatever the border settler-militiaman's shortcomings, he was capable of fairly prompt and oftentimes effective action.[12] Except for the British military activities in the French and Indian War, much of the defense of the frontier settlements down to 1783 was of local origin and substance.[13]

Wherever the Indian resistance to the spread of white settlements prevailed, the outlying areas were exposed to the ravages of what amounted to total war. Men, women, and children were equally endangered and victimized. The Indian early realized that settler occupation of the land was to become in fact total and permanent white possession of it. Consequently, he could not be selective in whom he attacked for two reasons: first, he was unequipped either by experience or source of supply to maintain the pressure of extended resistance, and, second, women and children were as great offenders to him as were men.[14] In fact, families coming onto the land signaled to the Indian the approaching of the end of his own access to it. Thus it was that in many areas of the frontier advance down to 1783 there were enacted a veritable succession of chapters of bloody and fiendish border encounters. Almost every new settlement underwent its fierce attack with its accompanying stories of death and torture. Yet, loose-jointed and disorganized as the citizen-militia force was, it formed a highly resistant human wall not only asserting an aggressive determination to occupy the land, but assuring safety in the future to its hearth and doorway.[15]

It can be said with assurance that the basic pattern of American pioneering was set by the end of the seventeenth century.[16] Whether it be the irregular river-oriented movement in the middle and southern colonies or the more or less orderly organization of towns on the New England frontier, the fundamentals of making a new settlement had been established. The earliest settlers who moved up the James to the fall line, or westward toward the Susquehanna learned to deal with the psychological force of isolation, to adapt to a bare subsistence mode of life, to make necessary adjustments in a heavily wooded environment, to subdue the land with main human force, and to explore the vast western littoral.[17]

Abraham Woods' adventures about the falls of the James were to be duplicated scores of times over before settlers reached the banks of the Ohio and Mississippi. The explorations of John Lederer, James Needham, Gabriel Arthur, Thomas Batts, Robert Fallam, and John Peter Salley were the forerunners of the subsequent exploits of Indian traders, long hunters, and land scouts of the eighteenth century.[18]

Repeatedly across the old frontier the adventurous Anglo-colonial woodsman was in the vanguard of westward expansion. He not only saw the land first, but he came into association with the Indians, spied out the course of the trails and rivers, and gathered invaluable topographical and geographical information. The famous Spottswood expedition of the Knights of the Golden Horseshoe which passed through the eastern defile of the Blue Ridges in western Virginia, in August and September, 1716, was only a more sophisticated land and geographical scouting party.[19] Although the term "long hunters" has been applied by historians to a specific group of third-quarter eighteenth-century wanderers and Indian traders, the practice was of seventeenth-century origin, and continued to be a fact in western expansion so long as there was virgin territory to be explored.[20] Out of this phase of American pioneering came many of the famous border heroes.[21] These Anglo-American wanderers were in many respects the counterparts of the famous French *coureurs de bois,* but they may well have been more forceful in their impact on the spread of white civilization. It is now all but impossible to disentangle the strands of history and to say how much of the long hunter activity was of private inspiration and how much of it was encouraged by speculative groups who sought to obtain prior knowledge of the location of desirable lands.[22]

Behind the initial explorations of the traders and long hunters came the settlers, an all-but-faceless horde which moved westward, opening tiny holes in the forest, establishing cabin-and-corn-patch claims to modest blocks of land, and planting a tenacious civilization. Only in the past century have many of these pioneering families achieved identity in the tracings of family genealogists.[23] Possibly there is no more significance associated with the spread of settlement across the virgin lands of the Old West than the restless movement of a relatively large number of near-impoverished yeoman families, many of which originated either as scions of indentured servants or indebted immigrant-ship passengers.[24] The American frontier was brutally demanding of human endurance of hard labor, privation, heartbreak, and the confrontation of dangers in a multiplicity of unpredictable forms. By the time the second wave of settlers had pushed inland from the eastern coast the process of advancing the Anglo influence along a widely dispersed frontier was sufficiently matured to establish it as a way of backwoods life.

It would be easy to generalize too much about the composition, the exceptional patterns of settlement, and the nature of humanity on the frontier. There were variations, of course, in the nature of the westward advance, many of them shaped by the conditions of nature and by the incidents of history. It is safe, however, to assume that the central movement adhered to a fairly consistent outline. One of the most remarkable aspects of the Anglo-American approach to the virgin West was that basically a highly individualistic movement achieved such a degree of social cohesiveness in moments of greatest need and on many occasions proved to be a powerful unifying force. At least three aspects of the human approach must be considered. First, the fusion of various national groups of emigrants into frontiersmen was little short of being a miracle in human association.[25] Second, the adaptation of men and families to the arduous labor, privations, and mysteries of the great woods coupled with constantly impending dangers revealed forces of human nature insufficiently understood and underestimated by British colonial officials. Finally, the yeoman settler in the western valleys of Pennsylvania, Virginia, and North Carolina moved onto the land to stay. He recognized no broad bounds of authority, and regarded his expenditure of effort and determination as the warranty price of his landhold. These were the people who were constantly on the move, penetrating new land barriers, ignoring the subtleties of colonial jurisdictions and even prior Indian claims.[26] The little pack horse-cabin settlers and the cattle-grazing squatters of the Old West were figuratively tiny human droplets which contributed to the confusion and erosion of the imperialization of the frontier. Their very mode of life was in fact a thwarting of formal authority, and continued to be all across the American borderland.

Whether pioneer settlers moved into new lands with warrants for grants or squatted without benefit of certificate they formed a tradition and a mode of physical occupation which was never substantially disrupted by future legislators and laws. The squatter became as much a fixed personality in the American westward movement as were the long hunters, fur traders, and land speculators. Just as important, they foiled the formulation of Indian policies which could be maintained and respected. The cravings for new lands were as virulent among them as it was among the companies and speculators.[27]

Despite the planlessness of much of the Anglo-westward human expansion in the first three quarters of the eighteenth century, it was not without its impressive institutional aspects. Transported in the meager social and cultural baggage of cabin settlers were the germs of several basic institutions which were highly adaptable to the sustenance of the spread of Anglo civilization.[28] One of the most important of these was that of common assistance, whether it be in the hasty raising of a cabin, slashing out a new ground in the forest, or the common defense of a new settlement. Throughout the entire pioneering era by Anglo-Americans, the common assistance principle was one of the most positive and sustaining domestic forces.[29] Politically the spread of the county system kept pace with the sprawling settlement line. This was one of the most remarkable contradictions in western American history. The county was a basic unit of the British governmental tradition, but on the frontier it operated as such largely in name only. The adaptations made in its form and the redirections of its purposes made of it a comparatively new institution. Actually it became a force of western political separatism. Present-day maps, of the older states, despite the frequent subdivisions of counties, still reflect the blanketing of broad areas with the semblance of this form of local authority.[30]

For the settler penetrating the land on a new frontier, the county represented a degree of security. It promised a certain amount of defense through the county lieutenant and a device for organizing a local militia; it registered deeds, recorded marriages, established a constabulary, and maintained a highly adaptable judicial process.[31] Virginia, for instance, filled out its territorial map with a veritable web of county boundaries which in time encompassed the region from the James River to Indiana. Once established the county became a monument of occupational permanence. Even beyond this it became an important link in the assertion of a central authority and the continuity of the Anglo-American governmental tradition. Significantly, the county in post-revolutionary years simplified the transition from outlying western territories into new states. Amazingly the Crown authorities and imperial policy makers seem almost to have ignored the political devices readily at hand in the practical management of their western affairs. In this area they left the responsibility to the colonial governors and legislators.[32]

For both the English and the French the Indian frontier with its internal tribal and national rivalries and complexities presented a continuing series of sensitive problems which did not lend themselves readily to the European mode of adjudication. The French made their own particular approach to dealing with the natives, and they seem to have experienced fewer difficulties than did the English. Their line of settlement, if in fact one existed, was of such a nature that it exerted no acutely discernible pressures against the Indian territories. They were able to integrate both their social and economic interests with those of the Indians more in the nature of infiltration rather than outright invasion.[33] They almost never encroached on Indian lands in the manner that the British colonial settlers entered them. Officially there was a fairly unified exercise of diplomacy and commercial relationships.[34]

The French, however, suffered one serious handicap; they could neither deliver trade goods in competitive quantities or at English prices, nor could they cope with the advantages of a great and gaudy variety of merchandise. The English had the ships, the mastery of the sea, and the shorter trade route. Behind their traders they had a growing factory system in the industrial revolution which assured not only an abundance of trade goods but that the volume of the western trade could be expanded.[35]

After 1740 the Indian trade was of major consequence in the process of Anglo-frontier expansion. The various colonial groups such as the New York, Pennsylvania, Maryland, Virginia, and Carolina traders penetrated the frontier from north to south, reaching all of the tribes east of the Mississippi.[36] In western Pennsylvania the famous Irish immigrant George Croghan not only established a thriving trade; he and his traders in unbelievably short time ranged over an enormous western territory in doing so. Beyond this, Croghan became a key Indian diplomatist, almost rivaling his superior, William Johnson. Traders who entered the Old Southwest, especially the sprawling valley of the upper Tennessee headstreams and southward to Mobile Bay, were just as aggressive in their pursuits of profits.[37]

Aside from its economic aspects the far-flung Indian trade resulted in the gathering of a productive amount of geographical, tribal, land, and distributive information, comprising a body of knowledge which the colonials drew on in the drafting of several important Indian treaties.[38]

By mid-eighteenth century the Indian treaty had become an established device for attempting to settle disputes and releasing blocks of territory for settlement. Three treaties, however, stand out as of major significance in this period. They were the Treaty of Lancaster which was negotiated in June and July 1744 to settle territorial disputes between the Six Nations and Maryland and Virginia; the Treaty of Logstown, June 13, 1752; and the Treaty of Easton, October 8–26, 1758. All three of these dealt with the French rivalry, the release of territory, the preservation of Indian rights, and permission for the British colonials to establish communication and commerce with the Indian tribes of western New York, Pennsylvania, and the Ohio Valley.[39]

The three colonial treaties established important precedents by which both the English, and subsequently the American government, undertook to placate their woods neighbors, to acquire blocks of territory, and to establish posts and settlements as forerunners of rising tides of settlement. The device of treaty making received a new impetus, and by 1780 it had helped to clear a considerable amount of territory below the Ohio of Indian claims. None of the treaties, however, even began to solve the ever-vexing problem of establishing identifiable boundaries which could be seen or protected. This problem was to be as disconcerting as any which disturbed Anglo-Indian relationships.[40]

In the whole complexity of Anglo-Indian associations three facts stand out. The Proclamation of 1763 was far more involved and complicated than most historians have made it appear to be. Not only did it attempt to close the Indian frontier for the moment to the speculator-trader-settler movement, but it sought to give the Indians temporary assurance at least that their territorial claims would be respected, and to concentrate the white population within a trading area in easy reach of the Atlantic Coast.[41] No document reflected more clearly the failure of London policy-making officials to understand the practicalities of conditions along the North American frontier. Viewed in many ways the Proclamation documented the failure and even the futility of trying to assess the demands of the western country from both Indian and settler viewpoints. Specifically, the advance of the squatter settlers into islands of the Appalachian frontier actually got beyond the bounds of such administrative control.[42] No fact was made clearer than the one that the Indian frontier could not be sealed off by the mere declaration of a muddled policy. To create an effective official barrier necessitated the presence of a permanent border military force which would enforce observance of the Crown policy from both sides of the line. Actually the Proclamation was defeated before it was issued because of the unbelievable blunders it contained.[43] The acquisition of such broad territorial areas as that involved in the Treaty of Paris, 1763, could not be managed without the creation of acquisitive pressures from settlers, suffering traders, and speculators. Nor could it be exploited without the exercise of a well-planned and sensitive Indian policy.

Animosities stirred by the Proclamation came as much from its psychological impact as from actuality of fact. It was clear that the British Government had devised no clear-cut Indian policy, and it was only bidding for time in which to develop one. The history of the drafting of the Proclamation reflects eloquently a lack of understanding of the nature and proportion of the needs of the western country at this critical transitional stage.

In like complexity the mismanagement and muddled western policies which led to the Pontiac Conspiracy and the other border incidents in the immediate post-French and Indian War years reflected the almost impossible task of maintaining a commercial and diplomatic relationship with the Indians, while at the same time trying to assert an authoritative control over their lands. The policies as administered by Lord Jeffrey Amherst were tailored to arouse resistance and conflict.[44] Not only was it a stringent policy as to conditions of trade, the sale of liquor, the distribution of presents, and prices paid for furs and skins, but it made increasingly clear to many of the Indians that they could not coexist with the English as they had done with the French without losing control of their hunting grounds.[45]

The establishment of the two regional Indian agencies or superintendencies by the Board of Trade, June 10, 1764, was a landmark of major importance in American frontier history. This decision had behind it a broad chapter of colonial trial and error, including the use of the agency concept. The governors in the Albany Congress in 1754, had urged the appointments of both a military commander for North

America and a separate military commander to take charge of Indian affairs.[46] The Board of Trade had seriously considered the creation of these agencies during preceding years, but the plan had not materialized. When the decision was announced under the title, "The Plan for the Future Management of Indian Affairs," it represented the ideas of several Americans including William Johnson, Edmund Atkin, George Croghan, and several of the colonial governors.[47] The "Plan" was detailed, comprehensive, and, in places, somewhat vague, but nevertheless it must be considered a major document in Anglo-frontier history. It was a basic attempt to formulate a broad administrative program for dealing with the all but insoluble Indian frontier problem. Too, it formed a precedent for later American efforts to deal with the same vexatious issues.[48]

In all the dealings with the Indians two tormenting issues confronted the British. First was the joint occupancy of the land, and second was the establishment of boundaries. This had been the haunting problem confronting the abortive Proclamation of 1763, and, as said earlier, accounted for the ill-conceived and arbitrary stipulation of the Appalachian watershed. The Northern Indian Agency was a sprawling and highly dispersed one. It contained forty-two tribes, representing about as wide a mixture of American Indian interests as could be imagined. It ranged geographically from the New York-New England frontier to the Illinois country, and only diplomatists such as William Johnson and George Croghan could have undertaken its management.[49] In the region below the Ohio John Stuart's Southern Agency represented thirteen tribes and again a remarkable diversity of human nature and interests.[50] Aside from the complications of Indian relations and communications were the complications of dealing with Spanish neighbors along the Gulf of Mexico. Stuart had both internal and external boundary problems. This fact is seldom defined in either the general histories of the republic or in those of the frontier, yet the issue was of major consequence and continued to be so until after 1830.[51] It was all but impossible to determine even general boundaries between the tribes because none had ever been formally established, and in order to adjudicate intertribal conflicts some type of boundaries or dividing lines had to be defined, and redefined.

Boundary difficulties were reflected in three main treaties. In 1768 the Six Nations agreed to relinquish possession of territory in New York, Pennsylvania, and Virginia, an estimated 40,000 square miles of land.[52] In subsequent treaties, Lochaber and Hard Labor, 1768 and 1770, the southern Cherokee ceded claims in western Virginia.[53] These latter cessions involved an extended discussion and negotiations over boundary locations. The proposals of the line wavered all the way from the headwaters of the New River to the mid-section of the south fork of the Holston.[54]

One further treaty must be mentioned. On March 17, 1775, the Transylvania Land Company under the leadership of Richard Henderson concluded the Treaty or Deed of Sycamore Shoals in which the Cherokee surrendered ownership of approximately 20,000,000 acres of land in present Tennessee and Kentucky.[55] This, and the three treaties mentioned above, opened the middle frontier to a flurry of speculative and settler activity. The Sycamore Shoals session fed a headlong rush of settlers through Cumberland Gap from Virginia, North Carolina, and the Watauga settlements into central Kentucky.[56] Likewise a movement down the Ohio took place.

Up to the Appalachian barrier, settlers had followed the river and Indian pathways. The frontier was far from being a trackless wilderness. There were Indian and game trails everywhere.[57] Few adventurers onto the old frontier were ever far from one of these trails. The long hunters had come through Cumberland Gap and had followed the great Warrior's Path part of the way through the Cumberland Valley. Croghan's traders had followed the trails inland on both sides of the Ohio.[58] Subsequently the land spies had entered the Ohio frontier by way of the paths, occasionally getting away from them and ending up in frustration and failure of their missions.[59] Thus it was between 1774 and 1780 several thousand settlers entered the upper Tennessee Valley and crossed over the mountains onto the Kentucky plateau. In quick order they established Harrod's Fort, Boonesboro, Logan's Fort, Bryan's Station, and Corn Island, and as quickly became victims of Indian raids from both the north and the south.

The early settlement of Kentucky created an entirely new stage of Anglo-American approach to the frontier.[60] First, most of the settlers who came into the land west of the mountains were already seasoned pioneers who for a full generation at least had become adjusted to the rigors of the frontier. No other western settlers had moved so far away from association with older settlements or well beyond the rim of Atlantic influences. Perhaps no other Anglo-Americans had so completely broken ties with the British and the old world. Too, no other American pioneers had been thrown so completely upon institutional resources of their own creation as were the Kentucky pioneers in the earliest years. They were almost altogether dependent upon their own resources for defense of their homes and fortresses.[61] They had moved away from ready communication with the legal institutions and had to petition for the establishment of a new blanket authority which was granted in the creation of Kentucky County in December 1776, and in the creation of three counties in 1780.[62] The Kentuckians were the first

Americans who had an opportunity to shape fully their political and social institutions from the outset of laying the foundations of what in a remarkably short time was to become an independent state. Too, they were the first frontiersmen to undertake their defense in a growing border conflict well away from the influences of the sagging imperial controls of Britain itself. These settlers had broken through all of the imperial barriers and now confronted the virgin land with a high degree of social and political independence born of conditions of the land rather than of the formalities of political declaration.[63]

Between the disruption of the founding of Harrod's Fort by Dunmore's War in 1774, and the final Indian skirmish at the Lower Blue Licks on August 19, 1782, the Kentucky settlements presented a paradox in human movement. With the possible exception of 1777, there was no year during the stringencies of the Revolution in which the stream of settlers did not continue to flow across the Appalachians and down the Ohio. During the grimmest moments of western Indian raiding the settlements continued to grow and the outlying stations to multiply. By the same token the beginnings of Kentucky came in time to form an anchor in the rear of the Revolution which saw both the Clark expedition into the Northwest and the internal resistance, such as the seige of Boonesboro in 1779, block what might have become a destructive back door action on the part of the British and Indians.[64]

In one other area the opening of the Kentucky settlements marked the closing phase of the old British imperial efforts on the frontier. The cession of land by the Cherokee to the Transylvania Land Company had little actually to do with Indian-white relationships. Both the Cherokee from the South and the Shawnee and related tribes from above the Ohio contested stoutly the occupation of the land, and it was not until after a second series of treaties, and two more wars, that they surrendered the territory. Also, there was left by 1775 in the new western settlement almost no trace of British land policies or the influence of the great speculative ventures which once had attempted to blanket the region with claims.[65] Basically this was the era of the little squatter claimant who undertook to hack out his landhold in the clumsiest of all methods of establishing physical monuments of ownership. This resulted in such utter confusion that not even the new state of Virginia could create legal means to make corrections. Subsequently Virginia passed two laws, in 1776 and in 1779, in an effort to correct the more flagrant failures of the western land system, but neither of these accomplished any appreciable order. Neither the land courts nor the civil courts in the following centuries accomplished this purpose.[66]

The settlement of Kentucky was simultaneous with the culmination of the British influence in the area. Nevertheless, the one and three-quarters centuries of British domination had left many deep marks on the frontier. The Indian problem was actually no nearer solution than it had been in 1740.[67] There remained all of the complexities of the western movement which the crown had attempted to solve in its various imperial acts. The failure of the central government to create a plan by which the orderly organization and administration of a new western colony could be undertaken in harmonious relationship with both the Indians and the colonial speculative interests was significant. For various reasons no satisfactory military organization had been created for the protection of the frontier and its inevitably expanding settlement line. Perhaps the most serious failure was that of the Board of Trade and other administrative agencies to comprehend that the resources of the North American frontier potentially offered the necessary source for capital for a greater imperialization of the region than all the Indian trade and land ventures put together.[68]

There was such a complexity of forces and counterforces at work that it is almost impossible to relate all of them to the central fact of the Anglo approach to the frontier. There were movements within movements. The larger and more visible activities of the central government and even of the colonial states themselves all but obscured the folk movement which gathered momentum after 1740, and certainly after 1763, to swirl and eddy in strategic puddles across the land to the Ohio.[69] There was possibly no understanding at all that one of the virulent germs which the pioneer settler carried west with him was that of separatism, a spirit which was to reflect itself repeatedly in the eddying of every new frontier settlement across the continent.

The Anglo-American approach to the frontier before 1780 was a movement of many strands. Interwoven in its fabric are the threads of stupid blunders, of victories, and of broad humanity. Above all the history of the early phases of frontier expansion was varied and complex. No period in American history saw the shaping of so many rudimentary patterns which were to bear upon the future development of so vast a region of virgin land. The nurturing of a completely western generation of aggressive settlers in the mid-eighteenth century presented a new aspect and a new challenge in the nature of the western problems which the Crown governmental powers neither perceived nor could solve. Yet at ground level the humble settler was the greatest potential force the British Empire might have used in the imperialization of the North American backwoods.[70]

Countless maps have been drawn to show the ambitious territorial inclusions of the speculative Loyal, Ohio, Vandalia, Indiana, Charlotte, and other land companies.[71] Yet none of these schemes succeeded. The historian of the frontier can only speculate whether or not they could have fulfilled their promoters' dreams, and if so what impact they might have had on the long range of the westward movement. There were, of course, land speculators who gained possession of large blocks of land, but in time most of these were broken up and had really no effect on the general progress of the frontier.[72]

The Crown government with its various ministries and boards was too unstable in the closing years of British control of the American colonial system to exercise efficient administration of so vast a continent.[73] Of importance was the fact that the internal rivalries and weaknesses of the ministries in the highly transitional moments of change prevented the formulation of any sort of administrative system which could have coped with the American problem. It was a singular coincidence of colonial history that the major pioneer breakthrough of the Appalachian barrier occurred during these years. Slow-moving and plodding though the pastoral westward movement may have seemed during the past century and a half, it had gained tremendous momentum after 1763.

There may in fact have been no solution to the Indian problem as it existed after 1740. Two cultures came head on with too many irreconcilable differences between the two. The land could not be equitably divided as to use so as to accommodate two such radically differing cultures. As a practical consequence of the mounting forces of the time one or the other had to retreat. The ultimate triumph of the pioneer advance was a monument to the tenacity of yeoman settlers, herdsmen, farmers, and traders, who made grass roots adaptations to the harsh conditions of border life before the seventeenth century ended. Their descendants who scaled the western ridges to spread out over the great internal valleys refined and enlarged the process of pioneering. They had come to respond to the rhythm of an expansive land well before the second Treaty of Paris became an official reality.

NOTES

1. Joseph Doddridge, *Notes on the Settlement and Indian Wars, of the Western Parts of Virginia and Pennsylvania* (Wellsburgh, Va.: Printed at the office of the Gazette, for the author, 1824), *passim;* Thomas Perkins Abernethy, *Three Virginia Frontiers* (University, La.: Louisiana State University Press, 1940), pp. 63–67; William E. Connelley and E. Merton Coulter, *History of Kentucky* (5 volumes. Chicago: The American Historical Society, 1922), I, 67–109; Thomas Pownall, *A Topographical Description of the Dominions of the United States of America,* edited by Lois Mulkearn (Pittsburgh: University of Pittsburgh Press, 1949), pp. 91–110.

2. Pownall, *A Topographical Description of the Dominions of the United States of America,* pp. 136–47; Philip Alexander Bruce, *Economic History of Virginia in the Seventeenth Century. An Inquiry into the Material Condition of the*

People, based upon Original Contemporaneous Records (2 volumes. New York: The Macmillan Co., 1907), I, 575.

3. John Smith, *The Generall Historie of Virginia, New-England & the Summer Isles with the Names of the Adventurers, Planters, and Governours from their First beginning Ano. 1584 to this present 1626* (London: Printed by I. D. and I. H. for E. Blackmore, 1632), p. 29.

4. Richard L. Morton, *Colonial Virginia* (2 volumes. Chapel Hill: University of North Carolina Press, 1960), II, 552–82; Alexander Scott Withers, *Chronicles of Border Warfare, a History of the Settlement by Whites of Northwestern Virginia; and of the Indian Wars and Massacres* (Clarksburg, Va.: J. Israel, 1831), *passim;* Lawrence Henry Gipson, *The British Empire before the American Revolution* (13 volumes. New York: Alfred A. Knopf, 1936–67), IX, 55–87; Clarence W. Alvord, *The Mississippi Valley in British Politics* (2 volumes. Cleveland: Clark, 1917), I, 168–82.

5. Samuel Kercheval, *A History of the Valley of Virginia* (Woodstock, Va.: W.N. Grabill, 1902), pp. 65–68; James G. M. Ramsey, *The Annals of Tennessee to the End of the Eighteenth Century* (Charleston, S.C.: Walker and James, 1853), map of Cumberland and Franklin, frontispiece; John Anthony Caruso, *The Appalachian Frontier: America's First Surge Westward* (Indianapolis: Bobbs-Merrill, 1959), pp. 103–22.

6. George Ranck, *Boonesborough* (Louisville: J. P. Morton & Co., 1901), pp. 19–35; William Stewart Lester, *The Transylvania Colony* (Spencer, Ind.: S. R. Guard & Co., 1935), pp. 78–80, 162–225. Some of the European-type forts are described in Jack M. Sosin, *Whitehall and the Wilderness: The Middle West in British Colonial Policy, 1760–1775* (Lincoln: University of Nebraska Press, 1961), pp. 111, 117, 168; Gipson, *The British Empire before the American Revolution,* IX, 92–94, 117–18.

7. Mann Butler, *History of the Commonwealth of Kentucky* (Louisville: Wilcox, Dickerman and Co., 1834), pp. 110–11; Connelley and Coulter, *History of Kentucky,* I, 183.

8. Excellent examples of backwoods fortifications were Fort Chiswell in Virginia, Bean's Station and Fort Loudoun in Tennessee, and Boonesboro and Harrod's Fort in Kentucky. Ramsey, *The Annals of Tennessee to the End of the Eighteenth Century,* pp. 175–208; Ranck, *Boonesborough,* pp. 16–39; Lester, *The Transylvania Colony,* pp. 79–82; John P. Brown, *Old Frontiers, the Story of the Cherokee Indians from the Earliest Times to the Date of Their Removal to the West, 1838* (Kingsport, Tenn.: Southern Publishers, 1938), pp. 67–74, 95; Robert S. Cotterill, *History of Pioneer Kentucky* (Cincinnati: Johnson & Hardin, 1917), pp. 94–95.

9. Morton, *Colonial Virginia,* I, 157–58; Lester, *The Transylvania Colony,* pp. 79–82.

10. The locations of these are displayed geographically on the "Map of the Cumberland and Franklin," as referred to in Ramsey, *The Annals of Tennessee to the End of the Eighteenth Century,* frontispiece; Brown, *Old Frontiers,* pp. 67–73. The latter work contains a double-fold map of the Cherokee country as a frontispiece.

11. There are literally hundreds of source references to this subject. One of the most graphic early ones is Withers, *Chronicles of Border Warfare, passim;* see also Chester H. Sipe, *The Indian Wars of Pennsylvania* (Harrisburg: The Telegraph Press, 1931), *passim.*

12. Withers, *Chronicles of Border Warfare,* pp. 114–20; Lester, *The Transylvania Colony,* pp. 162–96; Kercheval, *A History of the Valley of Virginia,* pp. 109–39.

13. Richard H. Collins, *History of Kentucky* (2 volumes. Covington: Collins &

Co., 1874), I, 17–24; Theodore Roosevelt, *The Winning of the West* (4 volumes. New York: Review of Reviews Co., 1904), I, 219–21.

14. Withers, *Chronicles of Border Warfare*, pp. 62–74; Gipson, *The British Empire before the American Revolution*, IX, 55–126; James A. James, *The Life of George Rogers Clark* (Chicago: The University of Chicago Press, 1928), pp. 51–68; Howard H. Peckham, *Pontiac and the Indian Uprising* (Princeton, N.J.: Princeton University Press, 1947), pp. 30, 39.

15. James, *The Life of George Rogers Clark*, pp. 51–68; Butler, *History of the Commonwealth of Kentucky*, pp. 41–48; Morton, *Colonial Virginia*, II, 686–90.

16. Abernethy, *Three Virginia Frontiers*, pp. 35–50; Josiah Stoddard Johnston (ed.), *First Explorations of Kentucky*, "Sketch of Dr. Thomas Walker" (Louisville: J. P. Morton and Co., 1898), pp. 3–4; Abernethy, *Three Virginia Frontiers*, pp. 29–62.

17. Kercheval, *A History of the Valley of Virginia*, pp. 45–55; Frederick B. Kegley, *Kegley's Virginia Frontier the Beginning of the Southwest the Roanoke of Colonial Days* (Roanoke: The Southwest Virginia Historical Society, 1938), pp. 11–47; Caruso, *The Appalachian Frontier: America's First Surge Westward*, pp. 24–42. Johnston (ed.), *First Explorations of Kentucky*, contains the journals of Thomas Walker and Christopher Gist.

18. Clarence W. Alvord and Lee Bidgood, *The First Explorations of the Trans-Allegheny Region by the Virginians, 1650–1674* (Cleveland: The Arthur H. Clark Co., 1912), *passim*, see particularly pp. 79–86, 139–71, 195–265.

19. Morton, *Colonial Virginia*, II, 444–53; Thomas P. Abernethy, *Western Lands and the American Revolution* (New York: D. Appleton-Century Co., 1937), p. 2.

20. Long hunting started with Batts and Fallam, Needham and Arthur, and later with Thomas Walker and Christopher Gist. The group to which this term technically was applied included John Finley, Michael Holsteiner, Kasper Mansker, Robert McAfee, Uriah Stone, John Rains, and Benjamin Cutbird. Connelley and Coulter, *History of Kentucky*, I, 160; Roosevelt, *The Winning of the West*, I, 172–209; Brown, *Old Frontiers*, p. 177.

21. Daniel Boone, Simon Kenton, Lewis Wetzel, John Sevier, Isaac Shelby, James Robertson, George Croghan, Christopher Gist, and John Donelson were some of them.

22. It seemed evident that Daniel Boone either represented or interested Henderson and his associates in his western adventures and the great tracts of virgin land he viewed. John Bakeless, *Master of the Wilderness: Daniel Boone* (New York: W. Morrow & Co., 1939), pp. 36–37. James Robertson's name was synonymous with the acquisition of western lands. Thomas E. Matthews, *General James Robertson* (Nashville: The Parthenon Press, 1934), *passim*; Brown, *Old Frontiers*, pp. 129, 178–85.

23. The bands of settlers who reached the Holston, Watauga stations, Boonesboro, and Harrodsburg were all but faceless so far as their personal identities were concerned. Ramsey, *The Annals of Tennessee to the End of the Eighteenth Century*, pp. 103–12; Connelley and Coulter, *History of Kentucky*, I, 160–69; Abernethy, *Three Virginia Frontiers*, pp. 63–69.

24. Albert Bernhardt Faust, *The German Element in the United States with especial Reference to Its Political, Moral, Social, and Educational Influence* (2 volumes. New York: Houghton Mifflin Co., 1909), I, 110; Morton, *Colonial Virginia*, II, 536–51; Harry Toulmin, *A Description of Kentucky in North America; to which are Prefixed Miscellaneous Observations respecting the United States*, edited by Thomas D. Clark (Lexington: University of Kentucky Press, 1945), pp. 12–23, 91–92.

25. Faust, *The German Element in the United States*, I, 361–90; Kercheval, *A History of the Valley of Virginia*, pp. 56–64.

26. Connelley and Coulter, *History of Kentucky*, I, 212–20; Cotterill, *History of Pioneer Kentucky*, pp. 58–70; Ramsey, *The Annals of Tennessee to the End of the Eighteenth Century*, pp. 140–74.

27. Abernethy, *Western Lands in the American Revolution*, pp. 3–13; Connelley and Coulter, *History of Kentucky*, I, 212–20; Samuel M. Wilson, *The First Land Court in Kentucky, 1779–1780* (Lexington, 1923), *passim.*

28. Caruso, *The Appalachian Frontier: America's First Surge Westward*, pp. 207–17; Arthur K. Moore, *The Frontier Mind* (Lexington: University of Kentucky Press, 1957), pp. 47–76.

29. Historical literature relating to the frontier is full of the treatment of this subject. The basic account most often quoted is Doddridge, *Notes on the Settlement and Indian Wars, of the Western Parts of Virginia and Pennsylvania*, pp. 261–86.

30. Samuel M. Wilson, "West Fincastle—now Kentucky," in *Filson Club History Quarterly*, IX (1935), 65–94; Withers, *Chronicles of Border Warfare*, pp. 46–47.

31. Wilson, *The First Land Court, 1779–1780, passim.*

32. The Crown government, of course, concerned itself with the large company requests for grants and those to individuals. The Transylvania grant, on the other hand, was acquired by deed directly from the Cherokee Indians, and the Watauga and Holston lands were occupied by permission of the governor of North Carolina. Most of the other early claims in Kentucky were derived from the same sources. Kenneth P. Bailey, *The Ohio Company of Virginia and the Westward Movement* (Glendale, Calif.: Arthur H. Clark Co., 1939), pp. 17–31; George E. Lewis, *The Indiana Land Company, 1763–1798* . . . (Glendale, Calif.: Arthur H. Clark Co., 1941), pp. 35–113; Ramsey, *The Annals of Tennessee to the End of the Eighteenth Century*, pp. 102–12; Lester, *The Transylvania Colony*, pp. 29–47.

33. John H. Finley, *The French in the Heart of America* (New York: Charles Scribner's Sons, 1915), pp. 120–25, 129–34, 150–58; Carl Wittke, *A History of Canada* (New York: Alfred A. Knopf, 1928), pp. 30–41; Gipson, *The British Empire before the American Revolution*, IV, 8–10.

34. Gipson, *The British Empire before the American Revolution*, IV, 4–9; Albert T. Volwiler, *George Croghan and the Westward Movement 1741–1782* (Cleveland: The Arthur H. Clark Co., 1926), pp. 55–113; Guy Frégault, *Canada, the War of Conquest*, translated by Margaret M. Cameron (Toronto: Oxford University Press, 1969), pp. 35–37, 268–74.

35. Gipson, *The British Empire before the American Revolution*, IV, 202–12; V, 62–63; Volwiler, *George Croghan and the Westward Movement*, pp. 33–54.

36. John R. Alden, *John Stuart and the Southern Colonial Frontier. A Study of Indian Relations, War, Trade, and Land Problems in the Southern Wilderness, 1754–1775* (Ann Arbor: The University of Michigan Press, 1944), pp. 20–37; Joseph S. Walton, *Conrad Weiser and the Indian Policy of Colonial Pennsylvania* (Philadelphia: G. W. Jacobs & Co., 1900), pp. 216–27; Bailey, *The Ohio Company of Virginia*, pp. 20–21, 204–206; Nicholas B. Wainwright, *George Croghan:Wilderness Diplomat* (Chapel Hill: University of North Carolina Press, 1959), pp. 22–46; William L. McDowell, Jr. (ed.), *Documents Relating to Indian Affairs, 1754–1765* (Columbia: South Carolina Archives Department, 1970), pp. xii–xiii.

37. Alden, *John Stuart and the Southern Frontier*, pp. 15–23.

38. Journals of Conrad Weiser, 1748, and George Croghan, 1750–65, in Reuben

Gold Thwaites (ed.), *Early Western Travels, 1748–1846* (32 volumes. Cleveland, 1904–1907), I, 21–44, 53–173.

39. Sipe, *The Indian Wars of Pennsylvania*, pp. 139–45; Gipson, *The British before the American Revolution*, IV, 252–54; Wainwright, *George Croghan: Wilderness Diplomat*, pp. 19–20, 49–50, 145–51.

40. Bailey, *The Ohio Company of Virginia*, pp. 125–44; Alvord, *The Mississippi Valley in British Politics*, I, 119–23; Alden, *John Stuart and the Southern Colonial Frontier*, pp. 273–76. This question was carried over in the United States' approach to the Indian frontier. Cyrus Thomas, "Introduction," in Charles C. Royce (comp.), *Indian Land Cessions in the United States* (Bureau of American Ethnology, *Annual Report*, 1896–97, Pt. 2, Washington, D.C., 1899), p. 583. Subsequent land-ceding treaties were Fort Stanwix, 1768, Hard Labor, 1768, Lochaber, 1770. Indian attacks continued on the Tennessee and Kentucky settlements until the 1780s. The Battle of the Blue Licks in Kentucky, August 19, 1782, technically ended attacks in this area. All across the Ohio frontier the attacks continued. "Narrative of John Brickell's Captivity among the Delaware Indians," in *The American Pioneer* (2 volumes. Cincinnati, 1844), I, 43–56. The Cherokee attacks in Tennessee and Kentucky were disruptive of the peace of settlers. Ramsey, *The Annals of Tennessee to the End of the Eighteenth Century*, pp. 143–47.

41. Gipson, *The British Empire before the American Revolution*, IX, 41–54; Alvord, *The Mississippi Valley in British Politics*, I, 183–210. The idea of containment of settlements to the eastern slope and trading area is expressed in *ibid.*, II, 131–32.

42. Kercheval, *A History of the Valley of Virginia*, pp. 45–64; James, *The Life of George Rogers Clark*, pp. 6–8.

43. Alvord, *The Mississippi Valley in British Politics*, I, 183–210.

44. Peckham, *Pontiac and the Indian Uprising*, pp. 70–93; Gipson, *The British Empire before the American Revolution*, IX, 105–13; Volwiler, *George Croghan and the Westward Movement*, pp. 158–64; Alvord, *The Mississippi Valley in British Politics*, I, 185–89.

45. Peckham, *Pontiac and the Indian Uprising*, pp. 70–73.

46. Edmund B. O'Callaghan (ed.), *Documents Relative to the Colonial History of the State of New York* (15 volumes. Albany, 1856–87), VII, 634–41. The evolution of the superintendencies is described in Alden, *John Stuart and the Southern Frontier*, pp. 139–55.

47. O'Callaghan (ed.), *Documents Relative to the Colonial History of the State of New York*, VI, 888.

48. "The Plan" was outlined in part by Edmund Atkin in 1755. His suggestions are contained in *The Appalachian Indian Frontier*, edited by Wilbur R. Jacobs (Lincoln: University of Nebraska Press, 1967), pp. 77–95; Wainwright, *George Croghan: Wilderness Diplomat*, pp. 207–209.

49. The full official text of this document establishing the agencies is contained in O'Callaghan (ed.), *Documents Relative to the Colonial History of the State of New York*, VII, 634–41.

50. *Ibid.*; Alden, *John Stuart and the Southern Frontier*, pp. 134–53.

51. Alden, *John Stuart and the Southern Frontier*, pp. 102–103; Louis De Vorsey, Jr., *The Indian Boundary in the Southern Colonies, 1763–1775* (Chapel Hill: University of North Carolina Press, 1966), pp. 228–34.

52. Thomas, "Introduction," in Royce (comp.), *Indian Land Cessions*, p. 584; Alvord, *The Mississippi Valley in British Politics*, II, 80.

53. Alden, *John Stuart and the Southern Frontier*, pp. 274, 279–81.

54. De Vorsey, *The Indian Boundary in the Southern Colonies, 1763–1775*, pp. 68–92.

55. Ramsey, *The Annals of Tennessee to the End of the Eighteenth Century*, pp. 117–20; Brown, *Old Frontiers*, pp. 1–13. The deed is presented in Appendix C of this work, pp. 553–56. See also Lester, *The Transylvania Colony*, pp. 29–47.

56. Lester, *The Transylvania Colony*, pp. 237–54. A list of Kentucky settlements and stations before 1780 is given in Connelley and Coulter, *History of Kentucky*, I, 200–10.

57. William E. Myers, "Indian Trails of the Southeast," in Bureau of American Ethnology, *Annual Report*, 1924–25 (Washington, D.C., 1928), pp. 729–854; Peter J. Hamilton, "Indian Trails and Early Roads," *Publications of the Alabama Historical Society, Miscellaneous Collections*, I (Montgomery, 1901), 422–29; Frank Wilcox, *Ohio Indian Trails* (Kent, Ohio: Kent State University Press, 1970).

58. Volwiler, *George Croghan and the Westward Movement*, pp. 32–38; Wainwright, *George Croghan: Wilderness Diplomat*, pp. 4–6.

59. Johnston (ed.), *First Explorations*.

60. Moore, *The Frontier Mind*, pp. 47–76; Connelley and Coulter, *History of Kentucky*, I, 160–99; Cotterill, *History of Pioneer Kentucky*, pp. 58–128; Lester, *The Transylvania Colony*, pp. 48–98.

61. The Kentucky pioneers emigrated from piedmont and valley Virginia, the Yakin Valley of North Carolina, and from middle and western Pennsylvania.

62. Collins, *History of Kentucky*, I, 19, 20; Butler, *History of Kentucky*, pp. 40, 118.

63. Abernethy, *Three Virginia Frontiers*, pp. 63–96.

64. James, *The Life of George Rogers Clark*, pp. 229–53.

65. Brown, *Old Frontiers*, pp. 208–24; Bailey, *The Ohio Company of Virginia*, pp. 285–93; Lewis, *The Indiana Land Company, 1763–1798*; Abernethy, *Western Lands and the American Revolution*, pp. 116–35.

66. William Waller Henning (comp.), *Statutes at Large, Being a Collection of the Laws of Virginia, 1619–1792* (13 volumes. Richmond, 1819–23), IX, 597, chap. XXIII; X, 97, chap. XXV; Wilson, *The First Land Court in Kentucky*, pp. 4–13.

67. An examination of Royce (comp.), *Indian Land Cessions in the United States*, reveals the tremendous energy expended upon treaties with the Indians for land cessions.

68. Englishmen far removed by space and experience from the natural scene of America could hardly have appreciated the great variety of resources or their economic potential. Being both conservative by nature and protective of the British industrial-mercantile system they may have had a practical point in attempts to restrict settlement lines with the Proclamation of 1763. Failure to appreciate the social and economic dynamism of the spreading American frontier was a key factor in British-American relations. There is a brief discussion of this fact in Gipson, *The British Empire before the American Revolution*, III, 280–81.

69. Lester, *The Transylvania Colony*, pp. 48–82; Ramsey, *The Annals of Tennessee to the End of the Eighteenth Century*, pp. 123–48; Cotterill, *History of Pioneer Kentucky*, pp. 150–76.

70. The backwoodsman might well have been the most loyal of the British subjects had the Crown pursued different Indian, land, and defense policies.

71. Lewis, *The Indiana Company, 1763–1798*, frontispiece; Abernethy, *Western Lands and the American Revolution*, pp. 39, 54.

72. Willard R. Jillson, *The Kentucky Land Grants* . . . (Louisville: The

Standard Printing Co., Inc., 1925), and *Old Kentucky Entries and Deeds* (*Filson Club Publication*, No. 34, Louisville, 1926), are perhaps the best published records of the disposition of lands in so broad an area.

73. Alvord, *The Mississippi Valley in British Politics*, II, 179–251; Gipson, *The British Empire before the American Revolution*, X, 367–85.